The Olympic Sports Economy

The Olympic Sports Economy

Max Donner

BEP BUSINESS EXPERT PRESS

The Olympic Sports Economy

Copyright © Business Expert Press, LLC, 2020.

Cover image licensed by Ingram Image, StockPhotoSecrets.com

First published in 2020 by
Business Expert Press, LLC
222 East 46th Street, New York, NY 10017
www.businessexpertpress.com

ISBN-13: 978-1-95152-700-6 (paperback)
ISBN-13: 978-1-95152-701-3 (e-book)

Business Expert Press Sports and Entertainment Management and
Marketing Collection

Collection ISSN: 2333-8644 (print)
Collection ISSN: 2333-8652 (electronic)

Cover and interior design by Exeter Premedia Services Private Ltd.,
Chennai, India

First edition: 2020

10 9 8 7 6 5 4 3 2 1

Printed in the United States of America.

Abstract

Every two years, the Olympics wins world attention with contests and celebrations. The success story of the world's most watched event, best recognized symbols, and most enduring brand has many valuable lessons for the business world. An entire constellation of talent and teams works behind the scenes to strengthen the Olympics and keep it relevant in a changing world. Veteran sports business journalist and MBA Max Donner gives readers a useful guide to the key success factors that make the Olympics an exceptional institution.

The Olympic Sports Economy incorporates exclusive case studies and reports from sports management conferences to illustrate the most important business practices and trends of the Olympics today. The text also reports objectively about recent controversies and challenges, as well as ways that readers can explore constructive solutions. *The Olympic Sports Economy* highlights the role the Olympics has played as a model for over six-hundred other international multi-sport competitions and introduces ideas from important trends in Olympic sports that can also benefit other organizations.

Contents

Foreword

by Steve Wilson, President Ex Officio Olympic Journalists Association

Whenever I reflect on three decades of reporting on the Olympic Games, the IOC, and the wider Olympic Movement, I always come back to one basic premise: The Olympics are the ultimate *global* story. No other sporting event matches the worldwide impact and international resonance of the Olympics or touches so many aspects of the world we live in: sports, business, industry, politics, entertainment, and more. The Olympics are much more than a 16-day sporting extravaganza; they are the lifeblood of a 24/7 multibillion-dollar sporting industry that stretches around the earth.

At the same time, the Olympics represent something that cannot be measured in dollars and cents, in television ratings, in commercial revenues, or in medal counts. They stand apart from other mega sports events such as the FIFA World Cup. They are held to a higher standard. They have a unique and magical quality. The Olympics stand for the values of excellence, friendship, and respect. They uphold the ideals of mutual understanding, solidarity, and fair play. They inspire. They bring the world together. They promote peace and international goodwill. As the late U.S. broadcaster Jim McKay put it, the Olympics constitute "the largest peacetime gathering of humanity in the history of the world."

I have had the pleasure of bumping into Max Donner at Olympic events around the world over many years. We've both witnessed the extraordinary impact that the Games can have on nations, on cities, on athletes, on institutions, on business, on everyday people. So I was fascinated to read *The Olympic Sports Economy*. This book provides a sharp and timely insight into the massive global scale and reach of the Olympic Games, the resilience of the Olympics in the face of so many challenges and their continuing relevance in today's world.

When the French educator Pierre de Coubertin founded the modern Olympic Games and the IOC in Paris in 1894, he could hardly have imagined that both would still be going strong 125 years later. Yet the Olympics have managed to survive through two world wars, crippling political boycotts, near bankruptcy, terrorism, and doping and corruption scandals. Coubertin would surely be surprised (perhaps shocked) at the size, scale, and commercialization of today's Olympics. But he would also be proud to see the way the Games have endured and remain pertinent, especially in today's increasingly divided and polarized world.

I recently asked the current IOC president, Thomas Bach, what was the secret to the longevity of the Olympics. He cited two main reasons:

> The first is that the values established by Pierre de Coubertin are still important, and are even more important in times of political and financial crisis. The second is that the IOC, in the most determining moments, always adapted to modern times and did not rely on tradition. That means keeping the values and holding the values high up, but also adapting the way we promote the values, how we interpret them, to a given time.

This theme of enduring relevance runs throughout *The Olympic Sports Economy*. The book provides a deep dive into the far-reaching impact of the Olympics. It describes how they serve as a foundation for the global sports industry and play an increasing role in the fields of health, human performance, and international communication.

Max delves into the economic realities and challenges that have scared off so many cities and countries from wanting to host the Games and raised questions about the long-term future of the Olympics. At this critical crossroads, the IOC has moved to revolutionize the bidding and hosting process. The focus now is on affordability, sustainability, legacy, and maximum use of existing and temporary venues. Building new arenas for the sole purpose of the Olympics is discouraged. The Games are being adapted to fit a city or region's long-term needs, not the other way around. The traditional bidding competition may be replaced by a targeted selection procedure. Future Olympics may be awarded to regions or multiple countries rather than a single city.

These reforms and changes will be felt all across the Olympic ecosystem. As the book highlights, this is a vast landscape: The Olympics have served as a model for more than 600 other international multisport competitions and institutions, providing a broad scope of social, economic, and sporting benefits supported by Olympic organizations, sports, and athletes.

Max traces the extensive reach of the Olympic movement through its network of more than 200 National Olympic Committees, dozens of continental and regional associations, and many international and national sports federations. This influence also trickles down to more than 1,000 grass-roots organizations of volunteers, nutritionists, fundraisers, and other specialists. This vast system combines to produce benefits that are, again, worldwide.

Like Max, I have personally observed and experienced the power of the Olympics from different perspectives and through many changes, from the 1980s up until today. As a journalist with The Associated Press, I covered 15 Summer and Winter Olympic Games and chronicled IOC Sessions, Executive Board meetings, and other Olympic events and stories across the world. I've witnessed Olympic competition from press tribunes, mixed zones, and training grounds. I've followed the behind-the-scenes politics, decision making, and controversies from conference rooms, convention centers, and hotel lobbies on all five continents.

I have witnessed scenes of unbridled jubilation and celebration when cities have won bids to host the Games as well as the tears and utter despair of those who have lost out after putting years of effort into their bid campaigns.

I have felt chills watching athletes from South and North Korea march together for the first time behind a unified flag in Sydney and seeing a trembling Muhammad Ali hold the torch aloft to light the Olympic cauldron in Atlanta.

I was exhilarated by the breathtaking performances of Usain Bolt in Beijing, London, and Rio de Janeiro, and the record-setting gold medal hauls of Michael Phelps.

I can still hear the explosion of cheers from the home fans when Sidney Crosby scored the winning goal in overtime against the United States to give Canada the ice hockey gold medal in Vancouver. When the puck flew into the net, the entire arena seemed to shake to its foundations.

It was a similar scene when Andy Murray served an ace down the middle on match point to beat Roger Federer for the London 2012 tennis gold medal on Centre Court at Wimbledon. The crowd erupted in a deafening roar unlike anything I'd ever heard at the All England Club.

Who can forget the feel-good stories of British ski jumper Eddie "The Eagle" Edwards and the Jamaican bobsled team? These plucky underdogs showed that competing against the odds with heart and determination embodies the Olympic spirit as much as winning medals.

There are also the little things behind the scenes that really endure. As a journalist, I have spent many hours sharing meals, riding on buses, and exchanging life stories with colleagues and new friends from all parts of the world. As a mentor for the IOC Young Reporters program, I have coached aspiring journalists from countries far and wide, from Barbados to Lesotho to Vanuatu. As a sports fan, I have marveled at the grit and passion of athletes from less developed countries who have dedicated their lives to making it to the Olympic starting line.

Some of my fondest memories go back to the 1994 Olympic Winter Games in Lillehammer. Many people had never even heard of the tiny Norwegian hamlet until then. But Lillehammer grabbed its spot on the world stage and left an indelible mark.

I can still relive the moments strolling down the snow-covered Storgata—the pretty main street—mingling with thousands of cheerful and friendly Norwegians of all ages, their faces painted in their national colors. Wherever you went during those two weeks, and despite the bitter Norwegian cold, the fans came out in force, not only to support their athletes but to cheer on athletes from all over the world. The fans turned the Games into a joyous festival of celebration, color, and sound. For everyone who was there, it was a magical, unforgettable experience that will forever be cherished.

And yet, not all Olympic experiences can be so pleasant. I will never forget the feeling of deep sadness and anguish upon confirming the death of Georgian luger Nodar Kumaritashvili in a training crash at the 2010 Vancouver Games. When I spoke with IOC President Jacques Rogge, he broke down in tears.

The tragedy brought home how the Olympics are about people, about humanity, about bringing the world together. It is that unifying global element which makes the Olympics so vital.

Acknowledgments

Conferences and Special Events

Event	Location and Date	Sponsor Organization
Sports Innovation Society	Paris, France June 6–7, 2017	Sports Innovation Society
Lighting and Hand-Over of the Olympic Flame	Olympia, Greece October 24, 2017	Hellenic Olympic Committee
Sport City	Lausanne, Switzerland March 7, 2018	SportCity
The Spot 2018	Lausanne, Switzerland May 15–16, 2018	Think Sport
ISPO Academy France	Paris, France September 14, 2018	eM Lyon Sports Management Program
Frankfurt Book Fair	Frankfurt, Germany October 10–12, 2019	Frankfurter Buchmesse
Follow Your Passion AiSTS Graduation 2018	Lausanne, Switzerland December 5, 2018	AiSTS
Olympic Games Broadcasting Exhibition	Madrid, Spain December 7, 2018	Olympic Broadcast Services
ISPO Munich	Munich, Germany February 4–6, 2019	ISPO

Team efforts are a sports tradition. It is fitting that there are many individuals who deserve recognition and thanks for sharing useful information and insights to put together the content of this book and make it easily accessible to readers.

There are several reasons that sports business and economics are not widely covered. One of the most important is the limited number of media accreditation opportunities. Sports journalists with extensive track records are rightfully selected first. Business journalists occasionally have opportunities for remaining slots. The extra efforts made by Nimtaz-Tanya Noordin of the IOC Press Office in 2009 and Madeleine Brennan at the Whistler Media Centre in 2010 allowed me to join other journalists in covering the Olympics and provide readers with more reports from the perspectives of economics and finance.

The individual most helpful in supporting my accreditation and providing an insider view of how the broadcast industry works is Marsha Bemko, Executive Producer of Antiques Roadshow in the United States. Together with her colleagues at WGBH, Marsha provided a nationally recognized accreditation and exclusive interviews that opened doors across the media industry.

Many other professionals have made extra efforts to secure invitations to provide an inside view of the sports industry: Anna Hellman, Stefane Mottaz, and Kevin Gabrielli at ThinkSport; Arnaud Drijard of the Sport Innovation Society; Aston Bridgman at the American Chamber of Commerce in Japan; Robert Gambardella of the Singapore Sports Institute; Dale Henwood of the Association of Sport Performance Centres; and J.C. Marchionni at the ISPO Information Center.

The first Olympic medalist to give me an exclusive interview and add insights from her business experience was Julia Mancuso. Many others followed and this book has benefitted in particular from the business school graduates—Phil Dalhauser, Gwen Jorgensen, Ous Mellouli, and Angela Ruggiero.

The IOC's own professionals have helped consistently by maintaining high preparation standards and recognizing the value the business media places on independence and objectivity. Christian Klaue at the IOC Press Office, Yiannis Exarchos and Catherine Philbin of the Olympic Channel, and Anne Chevalley of IOC Educational and Cultural Services have made great efforts to make sure that I and thousands of others who cover Olympics topics have good access to the information we need.

Case studies about the sports industry are just starting to be widely used. The contacts who arranged for access to content for the five new case studies in this text have made an important difference: Panos Giannaras of the Hellenic Olympic Committee, Nicolo Trambajolo and Vanessa Canone of ASI, Fulvio Martinez of Toronto 2015, Michael Schmidt and Valerio Cianfoni of World Baseball Softball Confederation, and Alexander Macheck at Red Bull Media.

I would like to extend very special thanks to the city of Baden-Baden in Germany, host of the 11th Olympic Congress in 1981. Baden-Baden reveres its heritage as an official Olympic City and made exceptional arrangements for me to have a convenient and affordable base to complete the research for this book.

Introduction

What is the Olympics? A showcase? A celebration? A sports spectacular? A competition? A tradition? A symbol? A foundation? A research institution? A scholarship program? A charity? A partnership? A franchise? A league? A community? A network? An innovator? A role model?

All of the aforementioned play an important role in making the modern Olympics work, but first and foremost, the Olympics is a foundation. It supports a global sports industry which generates over half a trillion dollars in revenues annually and is forecasted to double in size in the next decade. The Olympics' increasingly important role in the field of health and human performance is also improving health care expertise. And the Olympics has built a successful foundation for international communication.

The Olympic Games have also built the world's largest audience, reaching over 3.5 billion viewers. But coverage of the economic factors behind the Games is small by comparison. Charitable institutions from art museums to zoological gardens often de-emphasize finance because that is not their focus and they depend on volunteers and donors.

In the coming decade, the economic realities of the Olympic Games and the constellation of programs around them will have to get more attention because influential observers are questioning whether the Olympics will—or should—continue. During the 2018 Winter Olympic Games in February 2018, graduate students at University of Lyon's sports management program debated whether the Olympics will continue past 2040. At the same time, *Washington Post* columnist Robert Samuelson published an editorial with the provocative title "Will the Olympics Go Bust?"

This topic is as multifaceted as the Olympics itself. Expenditures to present the Olympics Games as audiences have come to expect often exceed $10 billion. There are ways to reduce and recover these expenditures. The World Masters Games and other events modeled after the Olympic Games have done this successfully. Less successful cases let

National Geographic publish a feature illustrated with former Olympic stadiums in ruins, an image far from Olympic ideals.

Regional leaders who build support for hosting the Olympics frequently cite the benefits of global attention, plus healthy involvement in sports for local residents, as long-term benefits. These benefits can stand on their own as success stories in Los Angeles, Barcelona, and Sydney showed.

But the main benefits of the Olympics are as global as the Olympics itself. The scale is so large and creates so much value that it is hardly visible when looking at a single 16-day sports event. Ways to heal injuries, treat chronic diseases, improve vision, increase energy efficiency, optimize hydration, and thousands of other valuable lessons have been learned from efforts to achieve success at the Olympic Games. This knowledge is shared widely in media ranging from medical textbooks to training programs for youth athletic coaches. These strengthen human resources and talent.

Olympic sports' contribution to preparing the workforce for future challenges deserves attention. Olympic athletes repeatedly demonstrate endurance, mastery of details and complex tasks, effective schedule management, focus on important goals, rapid adaptation of new technology, resilience, and engaging communications talent.

Partnerships with the business community enable millions of people to benefit from Olympic expertise. For example, Rossignol sponsors decorated Olympic winter sports athletes Martin Fourcade and Henrik Kristoffersen and works with them as technical consultants to develop high-performance products available to everyone.

The expertise developed in efforts to surpass past human performance has been important for more than a century. In the coming decade, as machines replace humans in a myriad of ways and pathogens evolve beyond the limits of traditional medical treatments, this expertise is becoming more valuable and may become irreplaceable.

An important element of the knowledge generated by the Olympics is truly unique. Each time a new world record is set, the world learns another aspect of the dimensions of human performance and gains better understanding of the factors that enable superior performance.

Serious discussions of how to finance the Olympics are timely and necessary. Humans have been building roads and bridges for thousands of years and over the course of history, the way these projects have been financed has changed greatly. An admired practice of top athletes and coaches should help focus these discussions. That is to break down an activity into its individual components and seek ways to improve each component. This book has just one goal—to enable professionals seeking to improve each component to do that important task even better.

CHAPTER 1

Building Values

Impossible Moments

"Impossible Moments, our new original series...features some of the most breathtaking, inspiring and unforgettable stories from the Olympic Winter Games—where the impossible happens." This promotion for the newest series on the Olympic Channel in 2018 highlights the spirit of the world's premier sporting event, the Olympic Games.

The modern Olympics has recorded a series of impossible moments. Some amaze, some inspire. In its entirety, the 125-year history of the modern Olympics has shown the world how to achieve new records and overcome old challenges.

Dutch road cycling racer Annemiek van Vleuten suffered a concussion and three cracks in her spine following a crash at the Rio 2016 Summer Olympics women's road race. The injuries landed the 33-year-old in intensive care. One year later, van Vleuten won the UCI world champion title in the same event and won again in 2018. She continued to compete to qualify for the 2020 Summer Olympic Games in Tokyo. The strength that she had built through two decades of training and the dedication she shared with many fellow Olympians enabled a spectacular recovery.

At the time of van Vleuten's tragic injury, the Olympics faced many challenges on its own course to the 2020 Olympic Games in Tokyo. Several of the international sports federations which manage Olympic qualifying events faced complex financial scandals which distracted from quality sports event management. The Olympics' "Zero Tolerance" policy against drug-based cheating in sports appeared almost unachievable as over 300 Olympic athletes were disciplined and medals were reallocated in a process that severely tested the ideals of the Olympic Movement.

At the same time, the Rio 2016 Olympics wrestled with a weak local economy and the dramatic impeachment of Brazil's former president. These issues made its ultimate success in presenting a traditional Olympics seem almost like a miracle. More and more cities, from Hamburg to Rome to Boston, considered hosting the Olympics and then backed away.

Two years later, the same strength and dedication that helped Annemiek van Vleuten get back on course to become a world champion had reinvigorated the Olympics with new optimism. FIFA contained the damage of financial scandals and presented a highly professional 2018 World Cup. Perseverance in holding drug-testing programs to higher standards began to rebuild trust. The Tokyo 2020 team was setting records of its own in building a stronger financial foundation for hosting the Olympic Games.

Olympic legend Andy Murray became a symbol for Olympic resilience with another inspirational recovery story. The Olympic gold medal winner of men's singles tennis tournaments in both 2012 and 2016 had announced in January 2019 that painful hip injuries had convinced him to stop competing in professional tennis. Just five months later, following a rigorous combination of surgery and physical rehabilitation, Murray was back in form and won the men's doubles tennis tournament with Feliciano Lopez at the prestigious Queen's Club tournament.

The resilience of the Olympic Games continues to impress people around the world and inspire many to pursue their own impossible moments. This strength makes the story of how the Olympics operate from day to day and year to year a set of valuable lessons about how to manage global enterprises and individual efforts.

The modern Olympics is not perfect. Its most dedicated followers know that all too well. But just like the ancient Olympics which inspired it, the Olympic community has literally changed the world for the better and become a showcase for the resilience and talent of the human race.

Numbers Count

A race from Marathon to Athens concluded the first modern Olympic Games in 1896. This "Marathon Race" became a brand name in the world of sports and emerged as a powerful symbol of what both the modern

Olympics and individual athletes could achieve. In 1896, 25 men from five nations started the race. The winner, Spiridon Louys of Greece, completed the 40-kilometer course in 178 minutes and 50 seconds.

In 2016, 155 men from 82 nations competed in the marathon race that concluded the Rio Summer Olympic Games. Of them, 140 finished the race and the winner, Eluid Rotich of Kenya, completed the 42.2-kilometer course in just 128 minutes and 44 seconds.

That 50-minute leap in performance equaled a 28 percent increase in speed in this grueling test of endurance. It made the iconic Olympic motto of "Faster! Higher! Stronger!" a reality and inspired millions of men and women to make these goals an important part of their personal lives. Over 1,000 community marathon races open to runners from around the world also took place in 2016. The largest, the New York City Marathon, reported that over 50,000 runners completed the rigorous race. Over 80,000 who met selective accreditation criteria applied for the New York City Marathon alone. London reported 247,000 applicants and Tokyo over 300,000.

The 2016 Rio Summer Olympic Games also featured a women's marathon that reinforced the Olympic community's commitment to sport for all with global participation and impressive results. Increasing participation by women in Olympic events has reinforced goals that appeal to spectators around the globe and keep the Olympic Games relevant. Engaging women in sports, a rarity 125 years ago, has been accompanied by physical fitness regimens and an increase in life expectancy.

In just one century from the Paris Olympics of 1900 to the Sydney Olympics of 2000, global life expectancy more than doubled to reach 66 years. Promotion of active, healthy living by Olympic sports was just one important factor in this success, but the status of the Olympic Games as the world's most watched event made it influential.

The iconic marathon races have also demonstrated the ability of the Olympic Games to include athletes from all nations and give all a good chance to excel. The 2016 medalists in the women's marathon represented Kenya, Bahrain, and Ethiopia, while the 2016 men's marathon concluded with medal victories for runners from Kenya, Ethiopia and the United States. Altogether, the 2016 Summer Olympic Games in Rio de Janeiro brought together 11,237 athletes from 207 countries spanning the globe. And 3.5 billion broadcast spectators watched them.

Both the 2016 men's and women's Olympic marathons shared an interesting distinction. All six medalists wore "Zoom Vaporfly" running shoes designed by Nike. This success added to timely discussions about the role of the Olympics as a human race following the ideal that victory must be based entirely on human effort. Over time, this ideal has become synonymous with the expression "level playing field," and given international sports organizations the challenging task of maintaining precise standards to define fair play for all.

For the business community, the impressive success of the "Zoom Vaporfly" runners at the 2016 Olympics highlighted other opportunities. This became one more visible way that elite sports promoted technological innovation and profitability. When the "Zoom Vaporfly" began sales to retail customers, its price of $250 commanded a large premium over average running shoes. This success story also showed sponsors adding expertise and not just money in sports projects. The success also contributed to Nike's goals for a related marketing communications campaign, branded as the "Breaking 2 Project." Its goal of enabling marathon runners to complete races in under two hours represents a 33 percent improvement in performance over the first Olympic Marathon victory in 1896. Not every advance of the human race reaches this level, but it is inspiring.

Another achievement of the marathon fitness culture inspired by the Olympic movement cannot be measured in minutes or dollars or percents. That is the inspiration and vision provided to individuals with chronic diseases who find rigorous athletic training regimens can improve their health and well-being. A frequent standout at the Chicago, New York, and London marathons is "Team Boomer." This is a charity founded to provide athletic scholarships to youth diagnosed with cystic fibrosis, a lung disorder which used to be fatal in many cases. Fitness regimens are now helping many individuals with cystic fibrosis live longer, healthier lives. In September 2018, a 31-year-old Welshman with cystic fibrosis named Josh Llewellyn-Jones set a world record in another Olympic sport, weightlifting. He lifted a total of 1 million kilograms of weights in one day.

Research by the University of Sydney in Australia has highlighted the value of sports regimens for good health. The cornerstone study of 80,000 adults began in 1994, when Sydney began planning for the 2000 Summer Olympics, and concluded 15 years later. The results presented very substantial reductions in the risk of death from any cause when subjects regularly exercised with one of these tested programs:

- 47 percent reductions for players of racquet sports—tennis, squash, and badminton
- 28 percent reductions for swimmers
- 27 percent reductions for aerobic exercise participants
- 15 percent reductions for cyclists

The conditioning of athletic training has other valuable health benefits. Regular exercise improves bone density and reduces the risk of fractures or chronic conditions that weaken bones. Studies at the University of West Australia School of Sport Science demonstrated that regular swimming regimens benefitted both the circulatory system and brain functions. The expanding field of sports science continues to find more ways that sports and exercise can improve health.

The Ten Billion Dollar Good Deed

The month before the 2016 Summer Olympics took place in Rio de Janeiro, a private investor group reached an agreement to pay $4 billion for the global UFC franchise in mixed martial arts. The price set a new record as the highest amount ever paid to acquire a sports franchise. That record did not last long. The month after the 2016 Summer Olympics, an even more staggering price level for sports franchises entered the record books at $4.6 billion, when Liberty Media agreed to buy the Formula One organization from entrepreneur Bernie Ecclestone.

The Olympics are produced by not-for-profit foundations and are not for sale. But premium prices paid for two successful global sports giants confirmed that the value created by international sports event producers is exceptional. This value is built on a foundation of a robust international sports industry with good growth prospects. The UFC deal set seven times gross revenues as an accepted premium for a successful international sports franchise, matching similar transactions in professional sports leagues. These benchmarks would make the commercial value created by the International Olympic Committee alone worth over $10 billion, based on forecast revenues of $1.5 billion a year.

New sponsorship agreements have reinforced the financial value of the Olympic Games. The combined value of two new multiyear agreements in the "The Olympic Partners" TOP global sponsorship program announced in January 2017 was $1 billion.

Highly sophisticated investors have validated multibillion dollar valuations for sports organizations. Computer billionaire Michael Dell joined the UFC acquisition syndicate. The Abu Dhabi sovereign wealth fund purchased 9 percent ownership of Formula One. The Olympics matches the success formula of Formula One and UFC: a valued franchise linked to a premium global brand. It is now benefitting from the value created.

The Olympic brand has earned gold medal status. A 2013 study by marketing experts at Sponsorship Intelligence, recruited by the IOC to conduct consumer research, showed that the Olympic Rings are the world's most recognized and admired trademark and that the positive brand image of the Olympics has a solid foundation. The 2013 study reported that the Olympic Games achieved the highest appeal and awareness ratings among 12,000 respondents surveyed in 16 countries.

The Sponsorship Intelligence study also underscored another important factor in creating a premium brand for which the Olympics ranks first worldwide. That is the scale of its global audience. This reached 3.7 billion viewers during the 2012 Summer Olympic Games. While that figure was almost half the world's total population in 2012, new ways to reach viewers on mobile devices are adding upside potential to the live viewing audience while new digital channels and social media are growing the capacity to rebroadcast Olympic events for viewing on demand. The forecast global audience for the Tokyo 2020 Summer Olympic Games is over 4 billion.

Gold medal championship status requires extraordinary effort to maintain and the 2016 Rio Olympics put this status to the test. A Spring 2016 study by Global Language Monitor observed the brand strength of the Olympics and its sponsors trending lower as media attention drifted toward the negative aspects of construction delays, budget woes, disciplinary challenges, and strained health care resources.

The success of new sponsorship deals agreed to after the 2016 Rio Olympics demonstrated that the Olympics had the resilience to maintain premium global brand status. The 12-year strategic partnership between the IOC with Alibaba Corporation of China announced in January 2017 was valued at $600 million in services and funding. That figure put a $400 million value on the eight-year global partnership concluded with Bridgestone Corporation of Japan a few weeks earlier.

This positive momentum helped the IOC to add another global titan to the Olympic Partners sponsorship program in June 2017. Intel, a pillar of the Silicon Valley technology community, signed an agreement to support the Olympic Games through 2024. The agreement illustrated important ways that this type of sponsorship agreement leverages the expertise of corporate partners to build unique competitive advantages for the management of the Olympic Games. These advantages, in turn, help the Olympics achieve goals of excellence and achievement that resonate with key audiences.

Organizing the modern Olympics has been a complex undertaking with complex challenges. Paying careful attention to fundamental values and promoting an idealistic vision has ultimately created billions of dollars in financial value. This has built a platform for creating more value in the future.

Traditionally, the fundamental Olympic values promoted have been excellence, respect, and friendship. As the Olympic Games have evolved and added new initiatives such as the Youth Olympic Games and the Olympic Channel, the values of fair play, sustainable growth, and promoting education have also grown in importance. These values are embodied in the Olympic Charter. It has served as a point of reference for thousands of Olympic community and sports organizations. Collectively, these initiatives and institutions have come to be known as the "Olympic Movement."

In practice, over a century, the network of organizations that has clustered around the Olympics has achieved admired success with a common strategy:

- Building on tradition
- Adapting to a changing world
- Providing leadership for the future

From Ancient to Modern, From Dream to Reality

The recreation of the ancient Olympic Games in the 19th and 20th centuries was so noteworthy that entire books have been written on the subject. The title of one, *The Idealist*, epitomizes the driving force behind it. This is a biography of Baron Pierre de Coubertin, the French fencer who organized the first Olympic Congress in 1894 and presided over the International Olympic Committee from 1896 to 1925. As the title suggests, this personal tribute portrays de Coubertin as a visionary idealist who inspired thousands of others to support his vision.

An important common foundation of both the ancient and modern Olympics was the principle of "sound mind, sound body." Originally popularized by the Greek thinker Thales of Miletus two centuries after the ancient Olympics commenced in 776 BC, the concept became a pillar of the Roman Empire hundreds of years later and helped the Romans structure institutions that functioned effectively across the many different regions which they ruled. The Latin phrase "mens sana in corpore sano" ultimately became a global ideal.

By the time Pierre de Coubertin realized his goal of gathering supporters at the Sorbonne University in Paris in 1894, this idealistic vision of promoting sound bodies and sound minds around the globe faced serious challenges. Farm laborers migrated to large cities with few facilities for staying active, imperialism had divided many regions, and sporting contests were often violent, raucous events. At the same time, for the first time, advances in transportation and communication had made it possible to organize international sports events as envisioned by de Coubertin and fellow founders of the modern Olympics.

Excavation of the ancient site of Olympia in Greece during the late 19th century fascinated millions with the legends of the ancient Olympic Games. Many texts describing the events, monuments, and history of the ancient Olympic Games made it possible to envision a revival.

Traditions of the ancient Olympics have encouraged success in the modern Olympics. Institutions, values, symbols, ceremonies, technological innovation, infrastructure, honors, and monuments all played an important role in the ancient Olympics. These inspired many aspects of the modern Olympics. And the modern Olympics has also followed the established practice of the ancient Olympics to adapt to changes in both the sporting world and international diplomacy to strengthen its status as the most prestigious sporting event.

Discoveries from the site of the ancient Olympic Games in Olympia, Greece, as well as hundreds of detailed written accounts of the ancient Olympic Games, created a valuable legacy for leaders engaged in the modern Olympic Games. Understanding how foundations of the ancient Games contributed to their extraordinary longevity has provided a frame of reference for impressive growth of the modern Olympics. In the ancient period, 293 Olympiads took place over a time span of 1,168 years. That is comparable to the longevity of the Byzantine Empire, the longest lasting institution in history.

Many institutions that supported the ancient Olympic Games have also become time-tested success factors for the modern Olympic Games. First and foremost have been universally agreed rules of competition. These have gone hand in hand with explicit prohibitions. Accepted practices and designated officials for adjudication strengthened the integrity of official rules and prohibitions. These were complemented by an accepted leadership body, the Hellanaki of Elea, the host region. These leaders also managed treasuries to pay for the Games and exercised authority comparable to the International Olympic Committee today.

The ancient Olympic Games found ways to balance tradition and the evolution of sports. Popular classical sporting contests took place again at each Olympiad: running races, long jump competitions, discus and javelin throws, wrestling, boxing, and the pentathlon. Other events were added or retired from the program in a way that appealed to spectators and made each Olympiad unique.

In addition, the ancient Olympics made a concerted effort to engage youth in sports and managed a series of separate contests for promising athletes aged under 18. The regular scheduling of the games every four years made it a milestone for each generation of aspiring youth.

The ancient Olympics incorporated many communal experiences which strengthened their appeal. Olympic hopefuls arrived from city-states throughout the Greek territories a month before the opening ceremonies. They lived together in shared accommodations akin to the Olympic Villages of today and trained together in the purpose-built

Gymnasium of Olympia. Pre-Olympic trial events were held to select the best athletes. This preparation also provided an opportunity for organizers to effectively communicate the rules, ceremonial protocols, and values of fair play they sought to promote throughout the Olympic Games.

The pre-eminent value promoted by the ancient Olympics was a dedication to continuous improvement. The ancient Olympic Games also promoted the values of inclusiveness as a foundation for high-performance competition. Originally, only male citizens from Greek territories could participate. After Greece was annexed by the Roman Empire, the community expanded to include citizens from throughout the Roman Empire. The Olympic values of fair play were reinforced by sacred oaths.

Preserving the history and achievements of the Games became both a value and a communications tool for enhancing the prestige of the Games. The disc of Iphitos, founder of the ancient Games, documented the Olympic Truce and other foundations of the Olympic Games and became the nucleus of a collection which ultimately filled an entire museum.

Athlete health and safety were high priorities in the values of the ancient Olympics. Very few athletes died in over 1,000 years of competitions and competition related injuries were rare. Athletes benefitted from a traditional diet of barley bread, oats, fresh cheese, dried figs, nuts, and lean meats rich in protein and vitamins. Modern sport dieticians continue to improve this facet of high-performance athletics.

Other scientific and technological innovations strengthened the ancient Olympic Games over time. Precision distance measurement devices and scales were refined for construction of the most advanced athletic facilities in the ancient world. A sophisticated measurement tool called a hysplex was invented to alert officials to false starts in races. Construction and renovation of stadia and amphitheaters employed sophisticated acoustical engineering so that thousands of spectators could hear announcements and competition results. This was just one dimension of the way that the demanding requirements of the Olympic Games became a stimulus to innovation and knowledge sharing. Today, innovation and knowledge sharing remain pillars of Olympic success.

A Universal Language and Dynamic Network

The impetus for the modern Olympics began with high ideals. The extraordinary effectiveness of sports in strengthening communications across borders and networking communities of talented people demonstrated many advantages. This helped to establish international sports as a universal language. Rapid advances in media from newsreels to television to omnipresent digital media made international sports images iconic. Ways the Olympics has highlighted the visual impact with dazzling imagery elevated international sports to a class of its own in reaching global audiences.

The trademark "Five Rings" logo of the Olympic Games is a case in point. Modern Olympics' founder Pierre de Coubertin sought to emphasize the universality of the Olympics and reinforce this value with a universally recognized symbol. Five interlocked rings, symbolizing five continents, stand out in color against a white background. Today, this iconic image of the modern Olympic Games is the single most recognized image in the world.

Universality has become much more than an Olympic ideal and has enabled a degree of global coordination that few organizations could rival on their best days. As in most Olympic endeavors, "perfect tens" are rare, but the efforts enable relatively smooth interactions within a network that has become a constellation of thousands of work units—national governing bodies, international sports federations, commissions, official broadcasters, local organizing committees, commercial subcontractors, volunteer groups, and many other support organizations.

This universal communication has been strengthened by the Olympics' ability to establish its icons as models for influential organizations around the world. The modern Olympics went a step beyond the olive wreath crowns awarded to victors in the ancient Olympic Games and began awarding silver medals to victors and copper medals to second place finishers at the Summer Olympics in Athens in 1896. Eight years later, the International Olympic Committee began the tradition of awarding gold, silver, and bronze medals for first, second, and third places. These awards became widely used symbols for excellence and achievement, adopted by most other international sports competitions and emulated throughout the communications profession.

While de Coubertin and fellow founders of the modern Olympics wanted to promote universality and universal symbols to promote Olympic values and human values, over time these created substantial commercial value. This has helped achieve the benefit of adding resources to support management of the Olympic Games and other programs in the Olympic Movement. Broadcasters, sponsors and communities make very large financial commitments to promote the Olympic Games in exchange for the valuable benefits of association with universal symbols, expertise, and excellence.

In the business world, the standards set by the Olympics have often become accepted as best practices. Teamwork, coaching, judging, and evaluation management systems frequently rely on expertise that demonstrated universal acceptance in the Olympics beforehand. This achievement makes a good understanding of the Olympics—how Olympic organizations work today and the vision of the Olympics for the future—valuable knowledge for business managers.

Testing Limits

Three-time Olympic skiing medalist Mikaela Shiffrin described her pursuit of Olympic goals as simply "I know no limits." Olympic legend Usain Bolt reinforced the view with his motto "I don't think limits." These aspirations are shared by hundreds of others who have reached new heights at the Olympic Games. But the impressive records achieved by Olympic athletes and their colleagues throughout the elite sporting world have not been easy and some impossible moments have been tragic or even fatal.

Only 10 athletes have died from sports-related causes during the Olympics over 120 years of competitions. But the frequency of death and injury in training or after competitions is a painful reminder that limits do exist and challenge the best intentions of sports advocates whose goals include promoting a healthier human race.

In late 2017, Olympic hopefuls David Poisson of France and Max Burkhardt of Germany died competing in the Skiing World Cup. While Mikaela Shiffrin was training for another successful gold medal victory at the 2018 Winter Olympics, English rugby player Ian Williams collapsed and died at training. And just after the 2018 Winter Olympics, boxer Scott Westgarth died from concussions sustained in a victory.

Four-time U.S. champion in open water swimming Fran Crippen never made it to the Olympics. He died from heat exhaustion in October 2010 following a competition in the warm waters of the Persian Gulf. The water temperature had been three degrees Celsius over the maximum allowed for competitions in swimming pools. The circumstances spotlighted the scale of challenges to promoting sports and fitness around a world that has many different environments for sporting events.

Noble, but tragic, death was also a theme in the athletic achievements of the ancient Olympic era. While the Marathon race has become the signature event of the modern Olympics, the heroic runner Philippides, who immortalized the original course, collapsed and died after finishing.

The strength and ambition of hundreds of Olympic champions has created margins of victory measured in hundredths of a second. And the controversies surrounding hundreds who risked their own health and the integrity of the Olympic Games with performance enhancing drugs to somehow gain that winning edge crossed more lines. This is testing the limits of the Olympics' own resilience as an admired global institution.

More sophisticated testing of doping control samples from the 2008 and 2012 Summer Olympics and 2014 Winter Olympics showed that a disturbing number of Olympic athletes had initially managed to hide prohibited levels of performance enhancing drugs. And more disclosures showed ongoing use of otherwise banned drugs by elite athletes who had successfully obtained waivers for therapeutic use. As of January 2019, retests using more sophisticated technology documented 86 drug code violations from Beijing 2008 and 116 additional violations from London 2012. Over 10 percent of the weightlifters competing at London 2012 ultimately failed more rigorous drug screening tests.

The drug retest reports did not include athletes such as Bradley Wiggins, who won a gold medal in men's cycling at London 2012 after exercising a therapeutic use exception for triamcinolone earlier that summer.

The complete dimensions of performance enhancing drug abuse related to Olympic competitions may never be known with precision. But the dozens of medals reallocated following more rigorous examinations and reviews could not avoid tarnishing the image of the Olympic community. Since six of the eight competitors in the men's heavyweight weightlifting event at London 2012 ultimately tested positive for doping violations, it became impossible to award three medals in line with Olympic traditions, an "impossible moment" far from the ideals of the Olympics' founders. And no solution appeared adequate to match the best Olympic ideals.

In addition to the many organizational crises that emerged in the sporting world, many athletes found themselves managing personal health challenges that were far from Olympic ideals, far from inspiring, and far from the goal of encouraging greater participation in sports and physical fitness. Fencers trained to lunge forward often developed muscle imbalances and strained tendons. A 2017 medical study showed measurably higher risk of death from cardiac arrest for triathlon competitors. Another medical study of NBA professional basketball players showed that 8.8 percent had missed games due to lateral ankle sprains over a 17-year period.

A decline in the number of cities making the effort to bid to host the Olympic Games sent a signal that Olympic organizations would need to address the root causes of negative perceptions in order to restore a strong foundation for the future of the Olympic movement. The race to host the 2016 Summer Olympics was the last to be rigorously contested. Four finalists were selected from a group of seven qualified candidates, with Rio de Janeiro ultimately winning over Madrid by a margin of 66 votes to 34.

The field of bidders to host the 2018 Winter Olympics and 2020 Summer Olympics narrowed to just three candidate cities. The competition to host the 2022 Winter Olympics saw one potential bidder after another withdraw from the race. Voters in St. Moritz, Switzerland; Munich, Germany; and Krakow, Poland, all opposed bidding in referenda. A parliamentary vote in Norway forced Oslo to withdraw.

Building Value by Building a Community

Collectively, the Olympic community is very large and creates exceptional value. The 105 voting members of the International Olympic Committee who lead the community and the over 13,000 athletes who compete in each four-year Olympiad cycle are literally the leading edge. Thousands of coaches, judges, referees, technicians, media professionals, medical experts, and other support staff are essential to presenting the games. On average, there are seven of these professionals for each athlete who qualifies to compete at an Olympics.

In addition, tens of thousands of volunteers make it possible to scale up for the logistical challenge of day-to-day operations when the games take place. Tokyo 2020 is trying to recruit 80,000, which would set a new Olympic record in another dimension. These kinds of efforts are matched by over 200 independent National Olympic Committees. Sponsors share their expertise by lending staff experts who also become integrated into the Olympic community. And many more talented individuals participate at hundreds of qualifying competitions leading up to the Olympic Games.

Then there are the spectators, social media followers, program participants, and global television audience. Over 2 million individual fans watched the 2016 Summer Olympic Games and Paralympics in person, purchasing 6 million tickets. The German Olympic Sports Federation serves 27 million dues paying members, and 43 million spectators viewed the London 2012 Olympic torch relay and Cultural Olympiad events. Hundreds of millions follow Olympic organizations and individual athletes on social media. And most adults in the world watch the Olympic Games as part of a global television audience.

The most engaged participants in the Olympic movement also attend related events such as sports demonstrations and ceremonies at Olympic gatherings or complete formal Olympic studies programs at universities and the International Olympic Academy. Olympic education strengthens the foundation of the Olympic movement and its values.

Education has also become a valuable factor in continuous improvement of athlete performance. Athletes and coaches observe top competitors and adapt their best practices. Olympic athletes train together in the Athletes Village. In addition, many Olympic athletes train together before Olympic competitions in global centers of excellence such as Hungary for water polo, Spain for cycling, and Canada for figure skating.

Video archives and additional educational programs organized by sports federations add to the choices for ongoing education. Massive online courses have extended the ability of Olympic organizations to prepare officials and provided a means to prepare large teams of volunteers to work together effectively. This kind of communication, in turn, reinforces the value of sports as a universal language.

The talent pool developed by this strong network of communication and participation programs has created a distinct competitive advantage for Olympic organizations to organize international sporting events. This kind of sustainable unique competitive advantage sets the Olympics apart and builds a foundation for future success.

No community this large can exist in a utopian paradise where problems never arise and no challenges exist. The talent pool that the Olympic movement has developed is a valuable resource for managing current and future challenges. The shared values of the talent pool contribute to frequent success. And the resilience that Olympic athletes demonstrate when they confront defeat or pursue an impossible moment also reinvigorates the Olympic community with new energy.

Key Sources and References

Information and observations in this text were compiled from interviews and conference participation as an accredited journalist as well as related news and sports publications. Results from Olympic competitions and

Illustration 1.1 The heritage of the ancient Olympics in Greece built a foundation for the modern Olympics and inspired its values.

IOC events are based on information published on the official IOC website, www.olympic.org. Other key sources are listed for each chapter. Where possible, financial figures originally reported in foreign currencies have been converted to U.S. dollars using prevailing exchange rates around the time period of the event or project discussed. The author recommends the sports industry trade publication, *Inside the Games,* for more detailed information about individual topics.

Boeckenhueser, T. February 2018. "Mikaela Shiffrin: Ich kenne keine Limits!" *SkiMagazin.*

Bull, A. 2019. "London 2012's 'Clean' Games Boast in Ruins as Failed Doping Tests Pile Up." *The Guardian*, January 8.

Butler, N. January 19, 2017. "Alibaba Group Announced as Olympic TOP Sponsor Until 2028." https://insidethegames.biz

Christian, S. 2017. "Revealed: How Liberty Media Bought Formula One." *Forbes.com*, August 15.

Croucher. M. 2012. "Death of US Swimmer Fran Crippen was a Disaster Waiting to Happen." *The National UAE*, September 14.

Drakos, M.C., B. Domb, C. Starkey, L. Callahan, and A.A. Allen. 2010. "Injury in the National Basketball Association: A 17-Year Overview." *Sports Health* 2, no. 4, pp. 284–290. Published online at https://ncbi.nlm.nih.gov/pmc/articles/PMC3445097/

Editors. October 1, 2018. "Cystic Fibrosis Sufferer Lifts One Million Kilograms in 22 Hours." *BBC.com.* Published online: https://bbc.com/news/uk-wales-45703545

George, H. June 2016. *The Idealist: The Story of Baron Pierre de Coubertin.* Ringworlds Press.

Intel Newsroom. June 21, 2017. "IOC and Intel Announce TOP Partnership through 2024."

IOC Department of Public Affairs. 2016. "The Fundamentals of Olympic Values Education."

IOC Newsroom. February 12, 2013. "The Olympic Brand Maintains its Global Strength and Recognition." Published online: https://olympic.org/news/the-olympic-brand-maintains-its-global-strength-and-recognition

Kevin, M. 2019. "Andy Murray Wins Queen's Doubles Title in First Tournament Since Hip Surgery." *The Guardian*, June 23.

Kim, T., S. Kil, J. Chung, J. Moon, and E. Oh. May 27, 2015. "Effects of Specific Muscle Imbalance Improvement Training on the Balance Ability in Elite Fencers." *Journal of Physical Therapy Science* 27, no. 5, pp. 1589–1592. Published online: https://ncbi.nlm.nih.gov/pmc/articles/PMC4483447/

Lawton, M. 2018. "Sir Bradley Wiggins' Use of Steroids Questioned by Former Team Doctor as Pressure Intensifies on Cycling Legend." *The Daily Mail*, September 23.

Longman, J. 2017. "Do Nike's New Shoes Give Runners an Unfair Advantage." *The New York Times*, March 8.

Merced, M.J. 2016. "U.F.C. Sells Itself for $4 Billion." *The New York Times*, July 11.

Michelle, A.B. 2018. "Annemiek Van Vleuten wins UCI Road World Championships 2018 Women's Time Trial." *Cycling Weekly*, September 25.

Morgan, D.O. January 10, 2018. "On Course for $10 Billion Quadrennium to End the Decade." https://insidethegames.biz

Peckham, D.J. June 15, 2012. "The Olympic Symbols and Protecting Sport's Biggest Brand." Published online: https://lexology.com/library/detail.aspx?g=86629961-0d5b-41c3-9f26-2295ab0b936a

Rapaport, L. 2018. "Triathlon Deaths not Rare, and Risks Rise with Age." *Reuters Health*, September 18.

U.S. National Institutes for Health. October 1, 2018. "Exercise for Your Bone Health." Published online: https://bones.nih.gov/health-info/bone/bone-health/exercise/exercise-your-bone-health

University of Sydney Newsroom. November 30, 2016. "Sports that Will Save Your Life Revealed: New Research." Published online: https://sydney.edu.au/news-opinion/news

Valavanis, P., and I. Trianti. 2011. *The Ancient Olympic Games* and *Olympia*. Papadimas Ekdotiki Editions.

CHAPTER 2

The MBA's Guide
to the Olympics

Learning From the Very Best

Building a ten billion dollar enterprise requires hard work, talent, dedication, and a long-term vision. The Olympics has moved forward with this approach and a foundation of two pillars of athletic success—cross-training and knowledge sharing. Olympic traditions have created good opportunities to learn new practices and adopt best practices.

Successful practices at individual editions of the Olympic Games demonstrated their value and became both enduring institutions and models for the rest of the sports industry:

- Marathon races made their debut at the first modern Olympics in 1896, stood out as a signature event, and have continued to win global audiences as the iconic closing event of the Summer Olympic Games ever since.
- The Olympic torch relay starting in Olympia, Greece, and concluding the official opening of each Games was introduced at the 1936 Summer Games. Afterwards, the torch relay became more than the commencement event of the Olympics. The relay became a model for international public relations countdown campaigns.
- The 1964 Tokyo Olympics introduced pictograms to visually distinguish sports and sports disciplines with memorable images which symbolized key elements of each sport. The 1968 Mexico City Olympics' design team built on this knowledge base to create pictograms which incorporated local

artistic traditions and became global trendsetters. Pictograms from the 1972 Munich Olympics employed uniform design rules and became the model for universally understood pictograms used at international airports worldwide.

- The 1972 Munich Olympics launched the tradition of Olympic mascots. This helped to engage more spectators and provide a simple, inexpensive way to participate in the Olympic experience. Subsequent Olympics have followed this tradition as part of sophisticated branding strategies.
- The 1984 Los Angeles Olympics demonstrated alternatives for financing Olympic host city programs from private sources. The strategic approaches of guaranteeing category exclusivity for corporate sponsors and organizing VIP and hospitality packages expanded at future Olympics and became mainstays of sports marketing as the industry matured.

The Olympic traditions of promoting excellence and adopting best practices have built a good foundation for positive feedback loops, epitomizing the popular saying "Nothing succeeds like success." Broadcasters value the Olympics as a showcase for leading edge technologies and formats. Live radio commentary of sports events began at the 1924 Summer Olympic Games in Paris, introduced by local broadcaster Radio Paris. The 1936 Summer Olympics was the first sports event broadcast on television and a testing ground for mobile and aerial cameras that helped to shape the future of sports coverage. The 1960 Summer Olympics inaugurated global sports broadcasting with jet delivery of videotaped coverage. The 1964 Summer Olympics marked major breakthroughs—transmission of color broadcasts and the first live international broadcasts using satellites. High-definition television (HDTV) made its debut at the 1984 Summer Olympic Games. More recently, the 2018 Pyeongchang Winter Olympics featured the latest 4K HDTV technology. This leadership has been rewarded with substantial premiums paid for broadcast rights and good sponsor relationships with technology companies Panasonic, Samsung, Alibaba, and Intel.

Similar positive feedback loops benefit the sportswear industry, a major source of sponsorship revenue for national Olympic teams and individual athletes. Good examples abound to show how benefits are leveraged as product innovations support high performance and good publicity. For example:

- Preparing for the 2010 Winter Olympics, Spyder Active Sports used wind tunnel testing to reduce the aerodynamic drag of ski suits by 15 to 20 percent. The company sponsored the U.S. Ski Team and outfitted downhill skiers with its most advanced high-performance wear. The team earned eight medals at Vancouver 2010, compared to only two medals at Torino 2006.
- 2016 Olympic women's triathlon champion Gwen Jorgensen and women's volleyball bronze medalist Kerri Walsh Jennings used Prizm Field sports sunglasses custom manufactured by Oakley. They credited improved depth perception with their excellent results.
- The Australian and New Zealand national sailing teams employed technological innovations from their sponsor Zhik. Its "Avlare" water repellent textiles weigh 75 percent less than wet spandex and improve sailors' comfort and range of movement. The Australian National Team tied with New Zealand for the most sailing medals won at the 2016 Summer Olympics, four each.
- Olympic TOP sponsor Samsung showed one more way that sponsors can add value by developing a training tool for Dutch speed skaters competing in the 2018 Winter Olympics. Uniforms embedded with electronic sensors transmit physical measurements of the skaters to coaches' smartphones during training for systematic analysis that helps optimize training regimens for each competition.

In addition, essential tasks of managing the Olympics have built specialized expertise:

- Coordinating Olympic qualifying events in many countries
- Working with National Olympic Committees (NOCs) and international sports federations

- Adding new sports and new medal events to Olympic programs
- Moving the Olympic program to different host cities
- Managing lists and databases of relevant resources

Olympic institutions are not perfect. On a recurring basis there are Olympic athletes who break rules and need to be disciplined and Olympic projects that exceed budgets and need to source supplemental funding. But these recurring challenges are matched by problem solving skills and resilience. These two traits are often important for athletic success and also build confidence that the Olympic Games will achieve its goals.

The modern Olympics exercises its core strength every day leading up to the games themselves. That strength is to develop human resources. Different Olympic sports require different talents and only a few dozen Olympians compete in medal events for different sports. But all Olympic sports share a common foundation of shared values and systematically train individuals to improve results and learn from high performers. That specific strength—learning agility—has established an impressive track record of success. The success is reinforced by scale. The 2016 Summer Olympics featured 11,384 athletes, and 2,952 competed at the 2018 Winter Olympics. That community of high achievers is large enough to find relevant case examples for most management challenges.

The learning agility promoted throughout the Olympic community has had a powerful impact on the world of business. Most people do not attend college. And many college students never receive any formal training in business administration. Often their relevant training in business management starts with sports for subjects like team organization and leadership, marketing and sales, statistics, and logistics. This makes the slogan of the Olympic Channel Podcast "Why not learn from the very best?" a management education mantra for millions of people.

The Gold Medal Brand

The Olympics' brand is the most widely admired in the world. It is also the oldest global brand in the world. The Olympic Games have been a symbol of aspiration and excellence since the first Olympic Games in

776 BC. Anthologies of Olympic history translated into Latin and other languages immortalized inspiring legends from the ancient Olympic Games. The signature symbol of the ancient Games, the victor's olive leaf crown, and other iconic images were widely replicated in coins, artwork, and texts which circulated through modern times and are displayed today in Olympic museums and prestigious ancient art collections.

The founders of the modern Olympics systematically enhanced the legacy and value of the Olympic brand with appealing imagery and sophisticated communications. The first Olympic Congress in 1894 introduced the iconic motto of the modern Olympic Games, "Citius, Altius, Fortius." This Latin phrase means "Faster, Higher, Stronger" in English and has been replicated as a popular saying in hundreds of languages as an inspirational call to action. Few iconic mottos can compete with the 125-year legacy of "Citius, Altius, Fortius." Three years after the first Olympic Congress, *The New York Times* began using its "All the News That's Fit to Print" motto, still used and still widely emulated today. DuPont's "Better Living through Chemistry" slogan remained in use for 65 years.

More recently, individual Olympics created inspirational mottos as cornerstones of their global communications efforts. The 2000 Sydney Olympics used the phrase "Share the Spirit" and the Beijing 2008 Olympics chose "One World, One Dream."

Three iconic institutions—the Olympic anthem, custom designed medals for each Olympiad, and ceremonies for opening and closing events—began at the first modern Olympics in 1896 in Athens. The 1896 Marathon race became an icon on its own and the signature final contest of each Summer Olympic Games.

Gold, silver, and bronze medals were introduced at the 1908 Olympics in St. Louis. Now other international multisport competitions use the same practice and iconic three tier podium stages, reinforcing the Olympic brand and the Olympics' status as a pacesetter. The choice of gold, silver, and bronze medals was subsequently adopted to distinguish high performance throughout the marketing communications profession. The International Business Awards, Advertising Age Magazine's awards for marketing campaigns, and, of course, the Sports Business Awards have all followed this standard.

Starting in 1912, custom designed posters for each Olympiad built anticipation for the Games and contributed to inspirational imagery. From the beginning, uniform images were replicated with texts in many different local languages. This made the modern Olympics a forerunner of global marketing campaigns.

The Olympic flag debuted in 1913 and launched the interlocked five rings of the Olympic logo on its course to become the world's best recognized design. Designed by Pierre de Coubertin himself, it represents the five continents of the world joined together in the unity of the Olympic Games. The color version uses five bold colors that project strength and vitality. The five rings imagery also graces Olympic medals, coins, stamps, sculptures, and engravings.

The many ways in which the motifs of the Olympic five rings have been customized for targeted communications goals underscore the symbol's power and endurance. The famous rings have been incorporated in signature logos of the individual Olympiads. The 1932 Los Angeles Olympics superimposed the rings over a stylized badge featuring the "Stars and Stripes" of the U.S. flag. Sydney 2000 placed the five rings below an image of an athlete racing in front of Sydney's iconic Opera House. Teams of dancers replicate the rings in ceremonies, pyrotechnic engineers project them with fireworks, neon artists illuminate landmarks with the rings, drone light shows project the rings in the sky, and over a hundred postal agencies have incorporated the rings in stamps.

The introduction of the first Winter Olympics in 1924 demonstrated the ability of the modern Olympics to extend its activities, and correspondingly, to extend its brand. The foundations of the same Olympic values and same icons as the Summer Olympics strengthened this effort. At the same time, the modern Olympics took care not to overextend its brand or mission and remained focused on producing the Summer and Winter Olympics during its first century.

Steps to Success

Inspiration from the ancient Olympics—and its endurance over a thousand years—has given the modern Olympics a good foundation. Adapting and enriching the program have strengthened that foundation.

Many key success factors of the modern Olympics have helped to make it a resilient and resourceful institution.

Collaboration skills have played a key role. Over time, the modern Olympics has built collaborative expertise that supports completion of very large projects. Collaboration leverages the capabilities of other organizations and partners. Managing many projects such as the Youth Olympic Games and the Olympic Solidarity scholarship program while interfacing with over 200 NOCs, plus international sports federations, broadcasters, labor unions, and many other groups, requires sophisticated persuasion and negotiation skills.

Not all leaders in the Olympic movement are former Olympic athletes. The IOC actively seeks experts in medicine, media, and other fields to work collaboratively in commissions and other initiatives. But 45 of the 115 IOC delegates with voting rights are recruited from Olympic sports, the NOCs, and International Sports Federations. And many of the 70 other voting delegates have had distinguished sporting careers.

Sports experience makes a difference. It is common in many sports for erstwhile competitors to become teammates and collaborate together. At Rio 2016, men's Olympic golf medalist Justin Rose of Team Great Britain defeated Henrik Stenson of Sweden by two strokes. But the two had been teammates together in the 2014 Ryder Cup and teamed up again after the Rio 2016 competition for the next Ryder Cup in September 2016 and once again in 2018. Roger Federer and Stan Wawrinka compete intensely at international men's singles tennis events. But together they won doubles competitions at the 2008 Beijing Olympics and the 2014 Davis Cup. And, of course, athletes of Olympic soccer, basketball, and ice hockey teams frequently play together with Olympic rivals on professional sports teams. Collaborative experience strengthens Olympic organizations when they move forward with large team projects.

In the Olympics, collaborative efforts typically start with relatively formal procedures for official recognition as an Olympic affiliated organization or sponsor. License arrangements are added when necessary. Ongoing management of team efforts also involves careful scheduling of conferences, selective invitations, extensive media promotion, grant programs, award programs, and other classic stakeholder management practices. Teamwork skills are a good foundation for these efforts.

The efforts required for 60 officially recognized affiliate organizations and 14 first tier sponsors are substantial.

The ways that Olympians learn to communicate also strengthen activities important for producing the Olympic Games. The international multilingual talent pool from which Olympic athletes are selected helps Olympians communicate more effectively with athletes and officials from other countries. Sometimes this involves gaining expert assistance, rather than acquiring multilingual skills individually. Eight-time Olympic medalist Kosuke Kitajima of Japan prefers his native language, but he has engaged translators and publicists to reach a global audience and build a social media following. This kind of experience is a valuable skill of its own.

In a 2018 interview, Pieter van den Hoogenband, a swimmer who won seven Olympic medals in the previous decade, explained how Olympic experience had developed his management skills. He described his experience preparing for international swimming competitions as comparable to being the manager of his own company, coordinating the efforts of many specialists, refining his management style, and building a team to support him. His perspective provided a useful reminder that there are typically seven to eight specialists working behind the scenes to master the details of participating in Olympic competitions—coaches, physiotherapists, dieticians, translators, and other talented individuals.

Olympic experience is particularly well suited to management challenges in the 21st century. Olympic athletes become accustomed to appearing on camera in settings that are often much more challenging than typical studios of routine radio and television productions. Many master interviewing skills as teenagers and leverage this experience to become interviewers and commentators after their athletic careers. Olympic athletes can attract social media followers and turn this into a platform for roles as social media influencers. And Olympic athletes are highly sought after as motivational speakers for good reason—they are admired for high achievement that required tough decisions and sacrifices.

A Robust Ecosystem

Many successful enterprises like Microsoft and Daimler-Benz have improved collaboration with ecosystems of services, research, training, and professional associations that provide more access to specialized skills and contacts. Over time, the Olympics has benefitted from an ecosystem of sports management expertise clustered around its headquarters in Lausanne, Switzerland, and strengthened by cooperation between Olympic host cities. And like Microsoft and Daimler-Benz, the Olympics also engages global networks of related organizations.

Fifty-five international sports federations anchor the local sports ecosystem near the IOC's own headquarters. The federations interact with specialized professional associations—the Global Association of International Sports Federations, Association of National Olympic Committees, Association of Olympic Sports Federations, and International Sports Chamber of Commerce, as well as headquarters and representative offices for international multisport events. WADA, the World Anti-Doping Agency, is headquartered in Montreal, but manages a state-of-the art testing facility in Lausanne.

The scale of having so many key players in the international sports field in one area has motivated dozens of other sports related businesses to locate offices nearby. Leading news agencies and sports specialty publications maintain branches for access to sports leaders and newsmakers. Public relations agencies operate nearby to facilitate media relations. Technology businesses and auditors assign their sports specialists to the area. In addition, nine area educational institutions have formed a consortium called the "Academic Network for Sports."

The proximity of so many sports leaders in one area has also made the region around IOC headquarters a global center of competence for sports legal and arbitration activities. The International Court for Arbitration of Sports and specialized law practices are located nearby.

The scale of having hundreds of sports industry leaders plus their staffs in one location also supports a wide range of sports industry events and continuing education programs. Each year, there are typically a dozen major international conferences meriting media coverage and several dozen specialized conferences which facilitate production of international sports events. These events keep participants well informed and project a professional image for the sports industry. This ecosystem also sustains a talent pool for special projects such as sports event bid evaluation and fundraising drives.

The highly structured relationship of the International Olympic Committee (IOC) with the over 200 NOCs has built a global extension of the sports management ecosystem. The NOCs have an exclusive right to select and manage teams of athletes from their respective countries for competition in each Olympic Games. The NOCs also oversee entourages of competent experts in health care, exercise, media relations, and other specialties to enhance team performance. The International Sports Federations that organize events in designated Olympic sports have an exclusive right to organize Olympic qualifying events. The value of these exclusive rights combines with the strength of the Olympics' brand and global scale to build unique, sustainable competitive advantages.

The Olympic ecosystem has tangible advantages. It helps to keep participants and experts well informed. It also helps many different sports organizations to reach agreements and harmonize positions on important issues like the introduction of new technologies for training or terms for category exclusivity in sponsor contracts. In turn, good agreements and quality communications in the ecosystem strengthen implementation when sports industry decision makers move forward with their plans.

The Olympic ecosystem has become stronger as classic competence centers emerged and aided acquisition of top tier skills by Olympic athletes. Eastern Canada emerged as a global center of competence for figure skaters. The 2018 men's individual gold medalist Yuzuru Hanyu of Japan and bronze medalist Xavier Fernandez of Spain both trained with Canadian Coach Brian Orser, an Olympic silver medalist.

Orser's coaching credentials also include 2018 Olympics double silver medalist Evgenia Medvedeva of Russia and decorated Olympic figure skater Yuna Kim of Korea. Orser's experience has demonstrated how elite athletes from different countries meet high standards and create a community. He has seen how they push each other and support each other, even though they are rivals.

Both the 2018 gold medalists and silver medalists in ice dance pairs also trained in Eastern Canada with the coaching team of Marie-France Dubreuil and Patrice Lauzon. Gold medalists Virtue and Moir are also Canadian and were joined by silver medalists Papadakis and Cizeron of France and 15 other figure skating pairs at this global center of excellence.

Similar athletic centers of excellence have emerged around the world and made world class training facilities economically viable. Ski jumpers train in Berchtesgaden, Germany, water polo players train in Hungary, and dozens of Olympic swimming competitors from around the globe have competed in USA Swimming's Grand Prix series. Aggregating talent and experience at a center of excellence promotes high performance and reduces training costs.

The Olympic ecosystem and Olympic talent pool also enable scalability. In the past decade, the Olympics has steadily added new programs that promote the Olympic movement and support Olympic athletes' professional development. The first Summer Youth Olympics took place in Singapore in 2010, followed by the first Winter Youth Olympics in Innsbruck in 2012. In 2014, the IOC launched an online Athlete Learning Gateway, followed by other initiatives to benefit athletes. The Olympic Channel began broadcasting in 2016. The first Olympic eSports Forum followed an Intel sponsored demonstration series at the 2018 Winter Olympic Games.

As Intel's expertise in organizing international eSports tournaments demonstrated, Olympic sponsors have a good track record of adding value. Cash contributions are essential to cover the costs of these large multisport events. But sponsor expertise, sponsor business contacts, and sponsor products offered as part of in-kind contributions strengthen Olympic sponsorship programs. Dedicated account management teams at the IOC and local host city organizers work to maximize this added value.

Multiple Streams of Income

The IOC is on course to average $1.5 billion in annual funding for its activities over the next several years. The individual sports events such as the 2018 Summer Youth Olympics and 2020 Summer Olympics manage separate budgets which fund activities on a much larger scale. The very large scale of global multisport events requires multiple sources of funding. While this necessitates additional effort and coordination, it also makes funding more stable and less reliant on the local economy or the profitability of an individual sponsor.

Fourteen prominent global brands support the first tier of commercial partners with the Olympic organizations in a program called "TOP: The Olympic Partners." The combination of business expertise they add gives the Olympics unique advantages:

- Alibaba, an e-commerce, online banking, cloud computing, and digital media conglomerate, based in China
- Allianz, an insurance and financial asset management institution, based in Germany
- Atos, an information technology solutions company, based in France
- Bridgestone, a tire and automotive components manufacturer, based in Japan
- Coca-Cola, the global leader in beverages for consumer markets with a growing franchise in sports drinks, based in the United States
- Dow Chemical, a manufacturer of sophisticated materials, based in the United States
- General Electric, a conglomerate with extensive health care diagnostic equipment operations, based in the United States
- Intel, the world's largest manufacturer of semiconductors and source of advanced technologies for the communications and broadcast industries, based in the United States
- Omega, a luxury timepiece and precision measurement equipment manufacturer, based in Switzerland
- P&G, a personal care and household products manufacturer, based in the United States
- Panasonic, a consumer and industrial electronics manufacturer, based in Japan
- Samsung, a cellphone and digital media producer, based in South Korea
- Toyota, the world's second largest automaker, based in Japan
- VISA, the world's largest consumer payment processing network, based in the United States

All of these commercial partners are well positioned for global leadership on their own in their product categories. Their collective support reinforces an image of global leadership for both the corporate partners and the Olympic organizations, a classic "win–win" outcome.

Many longtime sponsors accumulate expertise for key projects, making these commercial partnerships more effective. Coca-Cola has been lead sponsor of the Olympic torch relay a dozen times, starting at the 1992 Barcelona Summer Olympic Games, and signed up for an encore at Tokyo 2020. Its professionals are prepared to apply their past experience, test new features, communicate effectively with media channels, and help train local participants. And Coca-Cola's marketing professionals have learned more ways to integrate the torch relay into their global promotion of the Olympics. They also build lasting relationships with different communities from Olympic torchbearers to Olympic volunteers to Olympic memorabilia collectors.

The TOP sponsorship program is one of several ways that private enterprises help to finance the substantial costs of producing the Olympics. Sponsorships of NOCs, the Local Organizing Committee for each edition of the Olympic Games, and the Olympic qualifying tournaments organized by International Sports Federations add more resources.

Since there are over 200 NOCs, sponsorship programs range widely in scale and objective. Many global brands such as BMW, Adidas, Puma, and Nike sponsor multiple national Olympic teams and customize local campaigns to promote the Olympics. This frequently promotes internal knowledge sharing to optimize sponsorships. Nike engages product-savvy account managers who keep retail partners and the staff of Nike owned stores up to date about the features and benefits of their products and share knowledge for maximizing attention and sales potential from its different Olympic campaigns. Other NOC sponsorship programs give local sports business firms an opportunity for more global visibility. For example, Speedo, an Australian swimwear company, sponsors the Australian Olympic team, as well as individual athletes.

The Tokyo 2020 Olympics staff has achieved a remarkable sponsorship success story. Beijing 2008 and London 2012 both met targets for $1.2 billion in private sponsorships. Rio 2016 overcame a weak local economy to also raise over $1.2 billion in private financial support, thanks to a successful merchandising and licensing program that earned almost $400 million. Tokyo 2020 is taking private support to the next level. Two years before the scheduled start of the 2020 Summer Olympics, Tokyo 2020 had already recorded sponsorship commitments of $3 billion.

Most Tokyo 2020 private support is from first-time Olympic sponsors. Good results from their 2020 campaigns and sophisticated implementation of VIP packages could encourage them to extend their financial support at future games and add momentum to the Olympic movement.

Worldwide TOP sponsorship programs are well suited to global brands seeking high visibility worldwide. Sponsorship of individual local Olympics committees or NOCs offers a flexible alternative. The Adidas sponsorship strategy at London 2012 is a good example. Adidas invested UKL 100 million to sponsor and outfit London 2012 organizers as well as 11 national Olympic teams from important regional markets. This included outfits with the memorable Adidas three-stripe design for thousands of volunteers in addition to athletes.

Other sponsors find sponsorship of Olympic qualifying matches better for more targeted marketing communications objectives that also benefit from the gold medal brand status of the Olympics. For example, Longines has built a good marketing partnership with FEI, the international equestrian sports federation. This includes lead sponsorship of two prestigious Olympic qualifying events—the FEI World Cup and the FEI Nations Cup. Red Bull joined USA Basketball to sponsor Olympic qualifying contests for Tokyo 2020.

The phenomenon of "nothing succeeds like success" has made sports marketing the preeminent leader in the entire sponsorship category. Research by agency IEG showed that sports sponsorships accounted for 70 percent of all corporate sponsorship spending in North America in 2018. Another survey by the IMD Management School in Switzerland also showed sports attracting 70 percent of international sponsorship spending. The scale of the Olympics, Olympic qualifying events, and the 600 international multisport competitions modeled after the Olympics is an advantage that no other sponsorship category can match. Financially, this expertise is very important. The costs of promoting sponsorships and coordinating marketing campaigns are often three times the expenditures for each sponsorship.

Sponsorships and scholarships for individual Olympic athletes add another dimension to the Olympics financing formula. TOP sponsor Bridgestone also funds an athlete sponsorship program that reinforces its Olympic campaigns. It sponsored five athletes and one team at the 2018 Winter Olympics and celebrated a total of four medal wins. Sky Network, which broadcasts the Olympics only in New Zealand, manages an athletic scholarship program to cover top tier training and travel for 12 selected athletes competing in Olympic sports. Crowdfunding campaigns are becoming another financial resource for athletes. Crowdfunding site "GoFundMe" reported that 90 U.S. Olympic and Paralympic athletes raised a total of $400,000 before Rio 2016.

While the sources of financing available to the Olympics continue to increase, funding from broadcast rights and government investments in infrastructure have been essential. The IOC reported that broadcast rights accounted for 73 percent of total revenues for the four-year period from 2013 through 2016. The IOC contributed $1.374 billion to London 2012 to cover almost half of the local operating costs; the balance was funded by private sponsorships, merchandising, and event ticket sales. However, most bills for building infrastructure and security services were paid by the UK and London governments, which consolidated the expenditures with other government activities. Tokyo 2020 aims to reduce the dependence on government funds with the help of substantial private support and Los Angeles 2028 leaders plan private funding for all expenditures except security. This will make multiple streams of income all the more important.

Favorable Economics

Broadcasting industry dynamics have made the economic advantages of the Olympics more favorable by boosting revenues from broadcast rights contracts, the primary source of income for the IOC. When international television coverage of Olympic events began in the 1960s, broadcasters in many countries were government owned monopolies, while a small group of corporations licensed by government agencies dominated broadcasting in the United States, Japan, and a few other private enterprise economies. This limited the number of potential bidders for Olympic broadcast rights.

The growth of cable and satellite networks in the 1980s and 1990s brought about massive investments in privately owned broadcasting organizations and made it possible for sports networks to reach large numbers of households. Premium content, such as Olympic programming, enabled private broadcasters to acquire new viewers and cross-sell and upsell to existing customers. Premium sports content began commanding premium prices in broadcast rights negotiations.

By 2000, the increased number of channels supported by Internet communications and technical choices for archiving and rebroadcasting premium sports content worldwide made broadcast rights for premium content even more valuable. The revenues from the sale of broadcast rights reported by the IOC over the decades reflect this favorable development.

More recent advances in OTT (direct to viewer) systems facilitated the launch of the IOC managed "Olympic Channel" in 2016. This strategy is reinforcing the Olympics' ability to command premium pricing for broadcast rights by converting occasional viewers into regular viewers and offering sponsors additional choices for marketing campaigns. Olympic Channel sponsor Bridgestone demonstrated this with its 2018 Olympic athlete sponsorships and promotion of its Blizzak winter tires, which performed in tough winter weather throughout the 2018 Winter Olympics.

Favorable economic fundamentals of the Olympics have been strengthened by the convergence of sports business with related industries. Growing recognition of the contribution that sports and fitness activities can make to improving health care and treating some chronic diseases is fundamentally changing the health care industry.

In 2007, the American College of Sports Medicine launched an initiative called "Exercise Is Medicine" which expanded globally. Many university sports management programs are now managed by faculties of applied health science or are joint degree programs. Sports education leader Loughborough University has established a dedicated School of Sport, Exercise and Health Sciences. The newest large-scale sports management education program, The Indian Institute of Sports Management, created a separate postgraduate degree program for sports and health care management. Convergence of sports and health science is producing so much leading-edge research that a specialized industry publication, the *Journal of Sport and Health Science*, is now published quarterly.

Australia has significantly advanced the convergence of sports with health care. It supports Masters in Exercise Physiology educational programs at the University of Sydney, University of Queensland, University of Western Australia, Murdoch University, Deakin University, Victoria

University, and other institutions. Graduates accredited as exercise physiologists are officially recognized as health care professionals. Public health insurance and many private health insurance plans pay for preventative medicine and physical rehabilitation by exercise physiologists. Internationally, other universities have added similar programs, including German Sport University and the University of Delaware.

In the past decade, sports nutrition has grown from a specialized niche to a premium growth category within the food industry. Sports nutrition sales grew from $7.3 billion in 2011 to $11.9 billion in 2016 and are projected to grow 8 percent annually, according to market research experts at Euromonitor.

Digital media trends are also adding value to the Olympics and its partners. Success as an Olympic athlete has become a good foundation for social media audience growth. After the 2018 Winter Olympics, five-time Olympic medalist Martin Fourcade of France reached 450,000 followers on Facebook, 375,000 on Instagram, and over 250,000 on Twitter. This visibility reinforces achievements at individual Olympics and keeps fans engaged.

Digital media technology and cost-effective alternatives for reaching target audiences are also building an asset for many international sports federations. The International Equestrian Federation, for example, charges $79 for an annual subscription to FEI.tv and receives additional revenues for pay-per-view options.

Favorable economic trends for Olympic sports have an additional benefit. The increasing choices for financing an athletic career help Olympic athletes extend their careers and leverage their experience and fan bases. U.S. swimmer Mark Spitz won acclaim for winning seven medals at the 1972 Munich Olympics, but he went on to a career in dentistry and did not compete in future Olympics. Fellow American swimmer Michael Phelps competed in four Olympics from 2004 to 2016 and secured generous sponsorship support and fees for personal appearances to fund this achievement.

Olympic Sized Budgets

Favorable economics which have supported steady growth for the IOC and its ecosystem have been accompanied by steady increases in expenditures. The total cost of organizing and presenting the 1964 Summer Olympics in Tokyo was $72 million. The forecast for Tokyo 2020 announced in December 2017 was $12 billion. That reflects a compound annual rate of growth over 14 percent before inflation—or 11 percent a year adjusted for inflation—over the same period.

The 1964 Tokyo Olympics hosted 5,151 athletes competing in 163 events. Tokyo 2020 plans 10,616 athletes competing in 339 events, effectively doubling the scale. The increase reflects growth in the total number of countries participating in the Olympics, as well as an increase in the number of Olympic sports. Expanding worldwide participation in sports is an important goal of the Olympic movement, so Olympic supporters can view large budget increases as the price of success.

Comparisons with leading research universities can help put multibillion dollar Olympic budgets in perspective. The total expenses of operations, research, and financial aid by the IOC in the 2015–2016 period focused on the 2016 Summer Games and Winter Youth Olympics was just under $3.3 billion. That figure was very close to the $3.5 billion in expenditures by Yale University to support 12,500 students during an academic year in this period. The total number of athletes participating in the 2016 Summer Games and Winter Youth Olympics—12,604—was also close to Yale's enrollment. Both the IOC and Yale University spend about a quarter of a million dollars per participant in one-year programs and both are admired for quality education and research results.

Capital expenditures per participant in the Olympics and at Yale are also comparable. Total capital expenditure to construct an international campus for Yale at the National University of Singapore was $240 million for planned enrollment of 1,000 students. By this standard, capital expenditure of a quarter billion dollars per Olympic athlete looks competitive. The Tokyo 2020 capital expenditure budget of $3.2 billion is about $300,000 per athlete.

The long-term outlook for the Yale Singapore facilities and Tokyo 2020 facilities is somewhat different, but less different than a casual observer might think. The capital expenditures for the Yale University Singapore campus were planned for decades of future use. The 1964 Tokyo Olympic campus has been used for over five decades, and additional infrastructure for the 2020 Olympics will probably remain in use at least as long. In both cases, financial planners expect a "useful life" for these facilities of 40 to 50 years. After this period, the infrastructure will still be in place, but require substantial additional investments for modernization and continued use.

Both Yale and the IOC use subsidy programs to achieve their goals. In the 2015–2016 academic year, private foundations and corporations channeled about $200 million to support research and education at Yale. Private corporations and sponsors provide over $250 million a year in support of the IOC. In 2015 and 2016, the IOC awarded 1,547 scholarships for athletic training and equipment to Summer Olympics hopefuls, after awarding 440 scholarships through its Olympic solidarity program for winter sports athletes in the previous years. This total number of scholarships—1,987—is less than the 2,765 undergraduate scholarships which Yale awarded over the same period, but moving closer as funding increases.

Yale University and the Olympics share similarities in function and scope, as well as budgets. Both recruit and select talent globally for high achievement in competitive fields and foster learning agility. Both manage extensive portfolios of copyrights and licenses. And both stimulate innovations that improve commercial products and services and help advance public education and public health. Both the Olympics and Yale University have also encouraged partnerships of public sector and private sector institutions and provide training to work effectively in these kinds of partnerships.

Yale operates just over 100 different academic programs and three dozen departments. The Olympics manages over 100 different competition categories in 40 different sports and coordinates its activities with nearly three dozen different international sports federations. Both institutions reach out to experts and invest in conferences, publications, museums, libraries, and other communication platforms. This is expensive. And in both cases, many supporters have decided the investments are well worthwhile.

While the total budgets of the IOC and Local Organizing Committees for individual editions of the games appear large, comparison with other prestigious international events can change that point of view. The reported total costs for producing the Venice Art Biennale exceed 60 million Euros. That is approximately 150 Euros or 180 dollars per viewer. Total expenditures for producing the Summer Olympics now typically range from $12 billion to $15 billion. That range corresponds to less than five dollars per viewer. Prestigious international events that command global attention are expensive. The Olympics is no exception.

Do Olympic budgets need to be as large as they have been in the past? Probably not. A comparison with Loughborough University, a leader in sports management education, demonstrates how funding at different levels could work if necessary. Ranked fourth in the United Kingdom, Loughborough University's annual operating expenditures are just over UKL 250 million a year. That is about $350 million—$20,000 per student per academic year.

The $20,000 benchmark from Loughborough University resonates with the world of amateur sports; $20,000 a year is typically the minimum that amateur athletes need to budget to compete for a season in a wide range of popular sports from cycling to snowboarding that have modest equipment expenditures. Some other sports, however, are much more expensive. The budgets for medalists in shooting are often 150 times higher and winter biathlon costs are correspondingly high. So a substantial reduction in expenditures to produce the Olympics would probably require trimming expensive sports.

The feasibility of reducing Olympics expenditures could enhance confidence in the future. The 1948 London Olympics were often called the "Austerity Olympics" and managed to carry on the Olympic tradition with modest expenses. But from the perspective of business strategy, high expenditures help secure premium status. The Olympics needs to compete with other sports organizations for attention, talent, and financial support, just as leading research universities do. Olympic sized budgets have reinforced the preeminence of the Olympics and built unique, sustainable competitive advantages.

The Modern Olympics

The modern Olympics are just that, a modern event series. Inspiring traditions of the ancient Olympics and new traditions from the modern Olympics maintain audience loyalty. But the modern Olympics has had to master global trends to maintain its status as a premier program and sports industry trendsetter.

The 2018 Sports Analytics conference held at MIT's Sloan School of Business highlighted key trends that are redefining sports business, including the Olympics. Most topics covered featured technologies that did not exist outside laboratories a generation earlier. The Olympics' track record of incorporating relevant new technologies is good. But guiding future Olympics through today's communications and technology management developments is becoming a race on its own.

Many innovative sports technologies present helpful benefits that make knowledge sharing easier. Sophisticated studies of how athletes sleep, what exercise and nutrition regimens help optimize sleep, and even what fabrics best aid muscle recovery have become part of the tool kit available to high-performance sports institutes.

Machine learning in performance analytics, a recurring theme in sports technology circles, may also contribute to the level playing field ideal. Current research to improve injury prevention has good potential to support the "Athletes First" mission of Olympic sports and also encourage greater participation in sports. IBM is making versions of its "Watson Analytics" programs widely available to athletes and coaches. Some straightforward comparisons, such as tennis player performance on clay, grass, and asphalt courts, help both athletes and coaches focus efforts to improve performance.

Technology applications and business innovations are presenting new choices for attracting and engaging fans with corresponding financial benefits. Some approaches apply time tested economics and pricing models. These use data analysis to fine tune ticket packages and identify the communications channels fans like best.

The 2018 MIT Sloan sports conference also spotlighted technologies that Olympic sports organizations will need to balance with their traditional goals and values. Wearable technology has quickly advanced from visible monitors used in training to performance enhancing equipment that sports federations need to evaluate individually and may have to prohibit. eSports, portrayed as a "Showdown" with traditional sports at the Sloan conference, may attract and engage more fans to support sports. But some eSports could prompt a classic case of "market cannibalization." That is because eSports tickets and subscriptions may reduce personal budgets for traditional sports and some sponsors may reallocate their sponsorship dollars. And new ways that sports analytics can transform sports gambling will require all Olympic sports organizations to adapt.

As technology topics command attention in most of the sports community, Olympic decision makers will need to consider their implications and try to anticipate future trends. Emerging technologies present another challenge to the Olympic ideals of fair play and equality. They have the potential to transform many sports activities into expensive challenges in which wealthy players get a competitive edge. Grant programs like Olympic Solidarity may help level some playing fields, but it is not realistic to expect this funding to keep pace with the speed of technological change or with some cases of technology disruption.

Lead times for planning Olympic events are long—nine years between submission of bids, budgets, and business plans and subsequent presentation of the Olympic Games. And the trend has been for planning lead times to increase. In September 2018, Sapporo announced plans to prepare a bid to host the 2030 Winter Olympics. The short time frame in which many emerging sports technologies move from technical experiments to widespread practices is a game-changing challenge for Olympic organizations to maintain the integrity of the Olympic Games.

The Power to Inspire

Economics provides good reasons to be optimistic about the future of the Olympics. Growing sports audiences and participation gives the Olympics the added credibility of achieving important goals. Broader sports industry growth also benefits the Olympics by strengthening the financial foundation for infrastructure, education, product development, events, and institutions that support sports. Collectively, these support critical mass for a vibrant and self-sustaining business ecosystem, one of the most favorable competitive advantages any enterprise can achieve.

The Olympics also benefits from many other competitive advantages:

- A worldwide talent pool of experienced athletes and sports managers
- Strategic partnerships with sponsors and broadcasters who share expertise
- Financial stability
- A top tier brand reinforced by iconic images
- Exclusive image rights and licensing authority
- Effective models of teamwork for planning and executing complex projects

- Media and communications expertise
- Leadership in the growing sports industry, now reaching to health care and media
- Universal appeal that moves easily from country to country and sport to sport
- Forward momentum from past success, an advantage of the ancient Olympics for 1,168 years

Putting these competitive advantages to work has required agility, adaptiveness, and substantial changes. Many changes keep the Olympics in the news and relevant to many communities. The economic fundamentals of the Olympics make it likely that the next decade will bring more changes. Tokyo 2020 chose a fitting motto, "Get Set!"

A Case in Point: The Olympic Torch Relay

The Olympic torch relay has reinforced the prominence of the Olympics as a public relations pacesetter. The torch relay has also become an effective way to motivate many more individuals to embrace physical fitness and participate in Olympic community activities.

The first Olympic torch relay took place 40 years after the first modern Olympic Games, heralding the start of the 1936 Summer Olympic Games in Berlin. The flame was lit in a classical ceremony at the site of the ancient Olympic Games in Greece, with modern Olympics founder Pierre de Coubertin in attendance and literally passing the torch in his last major ceremonial role.

A total of 3,330 runners transported the ceremonial flame along the route from Olympia to Berlin with separate individual torches that became symbols of the Olympic movement for both the runners and their communities. At its conclusion on August 1, the Olympic flame was used to light an Olympic cauldron in the Olympic stadium, an inspiring ceremony that has been repeated and refined in successive Olympic Games.

Recent Olympic torch relays have focused on uniting communities in each host country and encouraging broad participation. Special events often capture spectators' imaginations with novel approaches such as submarine or scuba relays. Daily ceremonies build anticipation for the start of the Games and involve thousands of local supporters as performers and event volunteers. This foundation has also become a talent development resource for Olympic organizations, providing valuable experience to event and communications managers and training dedicated teams to works with sponsors, local communities, and the Local Organizing Committee which produces each individual Olympic Games.

Each edition of the Olympic Games features a customized design for the torch which attracts additional attention from spectators and the media. Tokyo 2020 selected a five-cylinder design inspired by the cherry blossom, a popular image in Japanese culture. The metallic finish also reflects the subtle tones of cherry blossom icons.

This single event series achieves many valuable goals:

- Linking the legacy of the ancient Olympics with the modern Olympics
- Promoting important social goals of the Olympic movement—inclusion, healthy physical activity, teamwork, and educating the world about the host country's culture and customs
- Strengthening Olympic community ties by engaging former Olympians and sports officials as torchbearers and ceremony guests
- Building favorable relationships with government and community leaders by inviting their participation as torchbearers and ceremony officials
- Growing the size of the Olympic community by engaging more spectators, event volunteers, and community event organizers
- Serving as a daily countdown program to the Opening Ceremony with a steady stream of media coverage
- Creating an historic legacy of each individual games with a large set of relay torches custom designed for each edition of the Olympics which are cherished by their owners and exhibited widely in Olympic and sports museums
- Supporting the goals of Olympic leaders in education by providing interesting subjects for student involvement and subjects for student projects

- Reinforcing the Olympic brand and imagery with millions of spectators' photos and videos shared across social media
- Building a talent pool that the sports community and sports media can recruit for future events
- Elevating the status of participation in Olympic events to an honor in the view of a large global audience

The success of the Olympic torch relay as a platform for strengthening a supporter community and building a large audience has been validated by frequent replications of this torch relay format at other important sporting events. The Asian Games, European Games, Pan American Games, and Special Olympics, as well as national sporting events such as the Canada Summer Games, have all incorporated similar torch relays and lighting ceremonies. The Commonwealth Games chose to add variety to the format with a baton relay. Each event aims to match the relay format to its own community. All benefit from the tried and tested approaches the Olympics pioneered by becoming the first organization to promote a torch relay to focus attention on a sporting event.

Illustration 2.1 Olympic traditions have created iconic images with universal worldwide appeal.

Key Sources and References

Fields, J. November 16, 2009. "Ski Suit, Designed by Boulder's Spyder, to Debut in 2010." *Colorado Daily*

International Olympic Committee, 2017, *IOC Annual Report 2016*

Newcomb, T. July 20, 2016. "How Oakley's Olympics Shades Could Help Athletes See Gold this Summer," *Wired*

Olympic Channel Podcast. 2018. Season One, Interviews with Brian Orser, Pieter van den Hoogenband

Sail-World.com editors. August 29, 2016. "Zhik sailors win 17 sailing medals at 2016 Olympic Regatta" *Sail-World.com*, published online

ThinkSport, 2018, *Lausanne Olympic Capital*, pamphlet

Today's Engineer Editors. August 2004. "Technological Innovations and the Summer Olympic Games." *Today's Engineer*

"Victoria University Master of Clinical Exercise Science and Rehabilitation curriculum," published online: https://vu.edu.au/courses/master-of-clinical-exercise-science-and-rehabilitation-amep

Wenn S., September 29, 2014, *Peter Ueberroth's Legacy: How the 1984 Los Angeles Olympics Changed the Trajectory of the Olympic Movement*, Taylor and Francis

Yale University Financial Report 2015-2016, published online: https://your.yale.edu/policies-procedures/other/financial-report-2015-2016

Yale University Financial Report 2016-2017, published online: https://your.yale.edu/policies-procedures/other/financial-report-2016-2017

CHAPTER 3

Accelerating Success: Olympic Sports Put Talent to Work

Sports, Education, and Entrepreneurship

When the International Olympic Committee held its 129th Session before the Summer Games in Rio de Janeiro, Nobel Laureate Muhammad Yunus presented a keynote address on the subject of entrepreneurship. While this marked a step in a new direction for a global organization whose traditional theme has been "sports, education, art," the new focus on entrepreneurship was both timely and a sign of things to come.

Two years later, the IOC announced the launch of the "Athlete365 Business Accelerator" in partnership with the Yunus Sports Hub in Paris. The partnership's goal is to encourage more entrepreneurship by athletes. The long-term potential for experienced athletes to promote innovations and strengthen Olympic sports is promising and Olympic leaders want to invest in that potential.

At the start of 2016, New York based Courtside Ventures launched an entirely new type of venture investment fund for early-stage investments in entrepreneurial companies focused on sports markets. The venture fund's initial capital of $35 million signaled a serious long-term commitment and gave the professional investment community greater confidence that sports related investments would merit attention. Eight months later, Microsoft announced the acquisition of one of Courtside's early investments, Beam, which customizes content for e-sports. Courtside Ventures also made investments in 16 other portfolio companies.

Global interest in entrepreneurship across the sports world accelerated. The LeAD sports business incubator in Berlin, also launched in 2016, received 840 applications for its second program, designed for a select group of 40 start-ups. Successful applicants start in a structured program with financial support, a shared workspace, management education, and helpful contacts with prospective investors and business partners. The influential founders are also the three grandsons of Adi Dassler, the German entrepreneur who launched the Adidas sportswear company 70 years ago.

The LeAD sports business incubator has become one of many. Paris, which hosted the first Olympic Congress in 1894, became home to *Le Tremplin*, an incubator designed for new sports businesses, in 2015. In the next three years, it supported close to 60 new ventures, achieving a success rate over 80 percent. Italy based Wylab was launched in 2016, received over 100 applications from prospective sports start-ups, and grew into a community of over 100 professionals in the following two years. Two sophisticated titans in the sports world, the Real Madrid Sports Club and Microsoft Corporation, joined forces to launch a sports innovation accelerator in Madrid, Spain, with the ambitious brand "Global Sports Innovation Center."

Across the Atlantic, Stadia Ventures launched in June 2015 in St. Louis, host city of the 1904 Olympic Games. Its plan envisions investing $10 million in sports related start-ups. In the three years after Stadia Ventures began its program, three of the companies, Winning Identity, Fishidy and Upgraded, were acquired at substantial premiums. And across the Pacific, Sydney, host of the 2000 Summer Olympic Games, became the home of the Sydney Sports Business Incubator. Located at the Sydney Olympic Park, it supported 20 companies in its first year of operations. These pioneer sports entrepreneurship programs validated the concept and encouraged others to follow.

Major league professional sports teams with access to large sums of capital for both early-stage investments and acquisitions of more advanced sports ventures took the sports entrepreneurship trend to the next level. The Los Angeles Dodgers MLB team, the NFL's Dallas Cowboys, and the Golden State Warriors and Philadelphia 76'ers from the NBA launched sports business incubators. All aimed to improve familiarity with emerging technologies that can enhance high performance in the sports world.

Indianapolis area teams chose a team effort to nurture sports business entrepreneurs. In 2018, the Indiana Pacers joined the Indianapolis Colts, two motorsports franchises, and the National Collegiate Athletic Association to launch the Techstars SportsTech Accelerator. This alliance of practical sports expertise is well positioned to evaluate the commercial potential of innovative sports technologies.

There have been enough "home runs" in the history of sports start-ups to merit serious attention from venture capital investors such as Courtside Ventures. The ESPN sports broadcasting enterprise was launched in 1978 with a $9,000 credit card advance and the time of its father and son team. After 35 years, the network was owned together by the Disney and Hearst corporations and valued at over $40 billion.

Investment returns at publicly owned sports businesses have been impressive. Nike's share price increase averaged 20 percent annually in the 25 years following its initial public offering in 1980. UnderArmour shares nearly doubled in the first day of trading when the company first went public in 2005. In the next 10 years, UnderArmour's share price rose 1,350 percent. These kinds of success stories distinguished sports business from mature consumer products industries whose historical growth rates have been lower than sports.

The robust growth that has made many sports ventures profitable investments should continue for at least another decade. Industry experts report that markets for both sports events and sports equipment have been growing at an average of 7 percent annually during this decade. That is double the rate of worldwide economic growth during the same period. In addition to strong economic fundamentals, popularization of sports in China and India, the world's most populous countries, has been adding momentum to sports industry growth. The Chinese market for sports products has been growing at 14 percent a year. Today, 2 billion people around the world participate in amateur sports on a regular basis, making sports one of the highest potential markets by any standard.

More Than Lifestyle Businesses

Nike, UnderArmour, and many other successful sports businesses were started by athletes with good business intuition. Nike was founded by

Phil Knight, a collegiate runner who recruited his track and field coach, Bill Bowerman, to launch the new venture while he continued working as an accountant. UnderArmour founder Kevin Plank was a fullback playing football at the University of Maryland.

TechnoGym founder Nerio Alessandri established the firm at age 22. It became the world's largest manufacturer of fitness and conditioning equipment. Alessandri credited his passion for sports with inspiring successful business concepts. Alessandri has built TechnoGym into a global company employing over 2,200 staff by promoting the wellness lifestyle. This vision was ultimately adopted by the World Health Organization as a standard for good health. TechnoGym has also been a model supporter of the Olympic movement, equipping the athlete training facilities at seven editions of the Olympic Games, as well as qualifying events such as the IAAF World Championships.

While Alessandri and many influential sports leaders have long promoted the wellness lifestyle, for decades, professional asset managers and venture capital investors shied away from businesses considered lifestyle businesses. Traditional investors viewed lifestyle businesses as mercurial and unpredictable. Decades of financial success at public companies like Nike and UnderArmour and at highly profitable private sports clubs such as Real Madrid and the Los Angeles Dodgers changed this perception. Sophisticated investors now see sports businesses much more favorably as dependable cash generators whose lifestyle characteristics build a foundation for customer loyalty, revenue growth, and premium pricing.

The credibility of sports business research at MIT and Stanford University, the world's top ranked institutions for science and engineering, has strengthened investor interest in sports.

When the MIT Sloan School of Business introduced its annual sports business and analytics conference in 2007 it attracted 175 participants. Attendance doubled each year and reached 1,000 in 2010, when ESPN became presenting sponsor. By 2018, the event was the largest student organized business conference in the world and over 3,500 sports business, technology, and investment professionals participated. Insights from sports influencers at leagues, teams, media firms, technology consultants, and equipment suppliers built momentum for sports business.

Knowledgeable sports industry experts do more than build confidence among investors that the industry has a bright future. They provide a reliable and credentialed talent pool for completing the necessary background research—due diligence—to move forward with investments and develop accurate forecasts and transaction values. In addition, MIT has organized an angel investing group to make early-stage investments.

Stanford's status in the sports world is different than MIT's, but also quite influential. Stanford won the Directors' Cup, awarded annually to the most successful overall intercollegiate athletic department in the United States, for 23 consecutive years through 2018. Stanford students and alumni won 270 Olympic medals through the 2016 Summer Olympics, ranking just behind the 309 medals earned by University of Southern California students and alumni, and surpassing the totals for Spain and Brazil combined.

Stanford is also considered the nucleus of the venture capital investment community. Over 90 percent of the investment partnerships in the Western Association of Venture Capital employ Stanford graduates.

The "nothing succeeds like success" element of Olympics and sports business has motivated innovative technology and health science research institutions around the world to make substantial investments in training bright, ambitious students for careers in the sports technology field. This growing talent pool gives professional investors added confidence that good business ideas in sports can become successful businesses with teamwork from capable experts.

- Loughborough University invested UKL 15 million (about $20 million) in its Sports Technology Institute. It is equipped to support design, develop prototypes, and test new innovations for improving sports performance.
- The University of Ghent Faculty of Medicine and Health Sciences opened a sports science laboratory complex named after former IOC Chairman Jacques Rogge in 2015. In addition to extensive research facilities for biomechanics, exercise science, and sports nutrition, the complex contributes to a commercial technology transfer program called *Victoris*.

- The University of Technology at Delft established a sports engineering institute with the goals of both improving performance and reducing injuries. Its extensive research agenda includes classic engineering approaches such as fabrication of new materials and precision measurement, as well as efficient architecture for sports facilities.
- Nanyang Technological University in Singapore operates three sports science laboratories, focused on human bioenergetics, applied sports nutrition, and performance measurement. Its research is strengthening development of medical treatments based on precision sports and exercise regimens.
- The University of Technology at Sydney established a Human Performance Centre to conduct leading edge research designed to improve athletic achievement.
- Southern Methodist University in Dallas, established a Loco-motor Performance Laboratory as part of its research initiative in human performance and added an Applied Physiology Laboratory; this research infrastructure supported the NBA Dallas Mavericks with applied sports analytics and developed an alliance with the team's owner Mark Cuban, a serial entrepreneur and private investor in sports businesses.
- Several university sports science research programs, including Yale, Ohio State, and the University of Texas, entered into a research partnership with the privately funded Gatorade Sport Science Institute and its satellite research laboratory at the IMG Sports Academy. IMG Academy is well positioned to transform research into practice with academic programs which train future sports educators and coach high-performance athletes, including many Olympic competitors. This research partnership is also accelerating the expansion of sports science in the health science field, distinguishing its researchers as sports health professionals.

Sophisticated research in applied sports technology is also encouraging additional entrepreneurial initiatives. The New York Sport Science Lab, for example, is building on the convergence of applied sports technology with the health and human performance field. Many of its programs can boost athletic performance and can also treat maladies caused by sports injuries or other health issues. Cryochambers use precision technologies for cooling to optimize muscle recovery. Superpulsed laser technology, approved for clinical use in early 2018, applies light energy to muscle tissues for better postcompetition recovery. The technology can also relieve pain without medication or side effects.

These kinds of initiatives benefit from the Olympic sports traditions of knowledge sharing, learning agility, and leveraging a talent pool.

Trendsetters

In the past century, the sports industry regularly leveraged the expertise of career athletes who transformed their insights on high performance into innovative products and designs. Professional tennis players and world champions René Lacoste and Fred Perry set high standards and track records of achievement for future athlete business founders.

Lacoste commercialized the metal tennis racket while still in his 20s and built a sportswear business for athletic lifestyles that was valued at over $200 million 90 years later. His success was also validated by the award of 20 international patents.

Fred Perry became a tennis legend by winning three championships in men's singles at Wimbledon. He became an entrepreneurial legend after he redesigned the sweatband and built a sportswear business using continued innovation to enhance sports performance. Sales grew steadily to reach $150 million a year 60 years later.

Lacoste and Perry were professional athletes and not eligible to compete in the Olympics, which was reserved for amateurs until 1984. In the current business friendly environment, more Olympic athletes are using their experience to start new businesses.

For some Olympic athletes, starting a company covers their expenses while they continue to train. Irish badminton player and three-time Olympian Scott Evans cofounded an upscale women's fashion enterprise in Denmark, where he has trained since he was a teenager. He manages information technology and social media programs to keep the firm growing at a healthy pace.

Fabiola Molina, who competed on Brazil's Olympic swimming team at the Sydney, Beijing, and London Olympics, is now promoting her passion for swimming with her own swimwear company. Molina's experience is reflected in product refinements that enhance comfort and athletic performance. Chlorine resistant *Aquos* textiles are reinforced with firm linings to optimize the swimmer's energy, and secure straps help minimize friction when gliding through water.

Other former Olympic athletes have resources to build businesses on a much larger scale. Gold medal winning skier Bode Miller is now part-owner and Chief Innovation Officer of Aztech Mountain. The company, founded in 2013, specializes in outdoor use sportswear which incorporates sophisticated materials and technologies. The young company now has retail sales distribution across the United States and in 10 other countries. It is well positioned in Tokyo, ahead of the 2020 Olympics, with 10 outlets.

Kerri Walsh Jennings, winner of four Olympic medals, including three golds, also has big plans for sports business. In 2018, the beach volleyball champion founded a sports digital media enterprise called Platform 1440. The business model envisions building a large audience with live streaming of fan-centric events, adding learning opportunities, and growing into a lifestyle brand. In July 2019, professional venture capital investor Theresia Gouw announced the partnership she leads would become a major shareholder.

Gymnastics Olympic gold medalist Anastasia Luikin is combining her athletic experience with professional management training to promote the Olympic tradition of knowledge sharing as a viable business model. "Grander" is both the corporate and product name. The program uses a foundation of fee-based workshops which Liukin organizes at major gymnastics events for general content. Custom training recommendations from athletes chosen by Grander's subscribers enhance the foundation. After validating the business concept in gymnastics, Luikin is engaging Olympians from other sports to grow.

The Grander business model has significant potential. It is scalable and generates recurring subscription revenues, two business success factors that professional investors favor. In addition, Liukin's own dedication to the Olympic value of continuous improvement can be a success factor on its own. Liukin did much more than train to win five Olympic medals at Beijing 2008 and multiple world championship titles. She served as the athlete representative on the Board of Directors of the International Gymnastics Federation and gained valuable experience as a board director of a multimillion-dollar international organization while in her early 20s. She then added professional management training in the sports management program at New York University, graduating in 2016.

Continuing Education

The modern Olympics, founded at the Sorbonne University 125 years ago, has continued to emphasize education. This started with classical physical education and evolved with the fields of exercise science and human performance. In 2015, the IOC launched an official Athlete Learning Gateway (ALG) with online versions of courses developed by University of Exeter, Deakin University, National Technology Institute of Lausanne, and other universities, as well as lecture series from industry experts.

The IOC ALG adds two important skill sets to the new entrepreneurship initiative. First, it provides professional training relevant to several high-potential product areas—sports media, sports nutrition, and sports medicine. Second, it introduces the fundamentals of establishing and financing a business start-up, as well as expert advice for managing a business, in its *Business of Sports* series. The ALG has also added an introduction to sports technology evaluation.

The ALG program emphasizes the competitive advantages that successful athletic training can transfer to business management and entrepreneurial efforts. The athletic traditions of dedication, perseverance, hard work, and passion are presented as foundations for a business career. The classic training and coaching practice of separating the key elements of performance to improve each step is presented as a good way of doing business. Coursework also encourages athletes planning a transition from sports to business to employ the extensive professional networks from their sports careers.

The steady growth of degree programs designed to train sports industry professionals, as well as more advanced executive education programs, has extended the talent pool. The first was launched at Ohio University in

1966, followed by the University of Massachusetts at Amherst in 1972. Ultimately, 400 other universities around the world followed this lead with professional sports business educational programs similar to the NYU program which Anastasia Luikin completed.

Growth of sports management education field has been an asset for entrepreneurial sports businesses from equipment and software providers to leagues, sports organizations, and sports broadcasters. In addition, the sports management education community responded to many new opportunities with programs designed for professionals to channel expertise into sports and promote the entire industry:

- In 1993, the University of Oregon established the Warsaw Sports Marketing Center, a research institute that enabled more sophisticated sponsorship and agency programs, boosting corporate funding for sports organizations.
- In 1998, Gutenberg University in Mainz, Germany, launched an Institute of Sport Science which also conducts academic analysis of sports business and forecasting.
- In 1999, the Birkbeck School of Management at the University of London established the Birkbeck Sports Business Centre with an infrastructure to independently evaluate complex challenges to sports administration such as match fixing.

In 2010, three additional university initiatives created new horizons for sports management:

- The Citadel Academy in South Carolina, opened the Dr. Hank Cross Human Performance Laboratory, following successful commercialization of materials research by Under-Armour.
- The University of Massachusetts at Amherst expanded its research programs in sports business administration with an endowment from IMG founder Mark McCormack. The research center has started an entirely new business case development program customized for sports business and is

also supporting training at international sports administration programs.

- The International Institute of Sports Management in India began a partnership with a private company, Eduhub, for more sports management training in India, the world's second most populous country. The program has been designed to encourage entrepreneurship and application of sports management know-how to the wellness industry.

Other sports management programs have also made significant investments in training sports experts to commercialize innovations. The United States Sports Academy (USAA), publisher of the influential *Sport Journal,* introduced a course dedicated to the essentials of sports entrepreneurship for graduate students. Since USAA also partners with sports academies in 65 different countries, it has significant potential to accelerate the adoption of entrepreneurial initiatives internationally.

Specialized high-performance sports institutes are also accelerating the transfer of sports management expertise. Worldwide, 88 centers of excellence for athletic training and sports science research operate and cooperate in a nonprofit association called the Association of Sport Performance Centers (ASPC). They help train Olympic athletes and many are managed by National Olympic Committees. Most will provide training and research support to athletes from other countries on a fee basis; they find that organizing training programs with top-level international competitors promotes quality learning and knowledge sharing. This high-performance sports community organizes regional and global forums which help circulate the most advanced findings throughout the sports research field.

Innovation at many sports management and technology centers of excellence has contributed to the growth of sports business. At the same time, the discipline of precision standards and uniformity demanded by international sports federations has often focused innovations and promoted quality control. The Sports Technology Research Group at Loughborough University adapted its research program for soccer balls used in the FIFA Men's World Cup from 2008 to 2016. This required meeting exacting standards set by FIFA for uniform quality. The final design incorporated advances in aerodynamic engineering and applied simulation software. It achieved both the primary goal of high performance during competitions and the important commercial goal of a 10-fold increase in the product's sales by Adidas, the company which sponsored the research.

The Tech Race

Teams in technology-intensive sports such as auto racing, sailing, and cycling frequently strive to keep their technology expertise secret with nondisclosure agreements. Olympic sports, which rely on international sports federations to set uniform standards and exclude technologies which could provide some competitors with unequal advantages, emphasize the Olympic tradition of knowledge sharing and the Olympic value of education. These different approaches often parallel the information technology industry, in which some enterprises, such as Apple and Qualcomm, work to keep their technology proprietary, while others, such as Microsoft, license technology to encourage innovation by outside developers.

The Olympic Channel is demonstrating how the knowledge sharing model can work in the sports field with its series called "The Tech Race." It features promising technologies to improve athlete training and reduce injuries, two fundamental goals of the Olympic movement. "The Tech Race" program also introduces several global centers of excellence in the sports technology field—the UK National Sports Centre in Bisham Abbey, Argentina's National Rowing Centre, the Biomechanics Institute of Valencia in Spain, and the P3 Sports Training Center in Santa Barbara, CA.

This sports science series shows how technological innovation can support in improving sports performance:

- Smart scales are providing a new way to measure athlete's jumps in key parameters which influence performance, including fatigue, and record the data for use by athletes and coaches to identify the most successful training techniques.
- Hybrid underwater + open air cameras with lens adjustments for different lighting conditions help coaches at Spain's

synchronized swimming team evaluate and improve swimmer routines with greater precision.

- Embedded sensors in Olympic rowing sculls measure the force, direction, and angle of all movements, as well as the boat's components beneath the surface of the water. Transmitting the data to portable computer devices helps to identify which combination of movements by individual rowers will optimize performance in varying conditions.

- Custom airbags, currently used for Alpine skiers, apply sensors to anticipate falls and inflate to protect athletes from injuries. This technology also stores the data from each run to create software-defined guides to reduce risk of injury. This kind of technology, first conceived for the needs of high-performance athletes, could also reduce injuries of emergency response teams and other rescue professionals and bring sports innovation to the health care industry.

Using wind tunnel aerodynamic practice sessions as part of athletic training is showing how high-tech research facilities can add value across a wide range of sports. Performance in bobsled, luge, windsurfing, and most outdoor sports can be modeled more precisely in the controlled conditions of industrial wind tunnels. Some are operated by companies such as Audi and BMW which sponsor international sports federations or National Olympic Committees, while others are located at research universities making progress in sports science.

Sports technology is also demonstrating the power of research and development for sophisticated new materials. Carbon fiber, for example, has made an impressive difference. Pole vaulters at the first modern Olympics in 1896 used bamboo poles that weighed 10 kilograms. Today's competitors use carbon fiber poles that weigh 80 percent less. This improvement transfers into more energy for each pole vault. The Olympic men's pole vault record of 6.03 meters set at Rio 2016 was almost twice the 3.3-meter gold medal standard in the same event at the first modern Olympics in 1896.

Carbon fiber innovations are also being used for sports equipment that can be redesigned for the health care and physical rehabilitation industries. Prosthetic carbon fiber springs used by amputees competing in Paralympic races can also be modified to enable many other amputees to benefit from improved mobility. And in the future, more innovations may offer alternatives for strained or injured ankle and knee joints.

There are also marketing and financial management dimensions to sports technology innovation. Equipment upgrades increase revenues which, in turn, can be used to fund future research and development. Athletes and teams have good reasons to trade up to the most current version of equipment for their sports, and ideally donate their used equipment to schools. Thoughtful donations can help increase the size of the total market for the equipment category.

Leading edge innovations developed for high-performance Olympic athletes often depend on custom manufacturing of small lots and are correspondingly expensive. Successful proof of concept in Olympic sports and persuasive athlete endorsements improve the economics of mass production. This way, innovations originally stimulated by Olympic qualifying events and competitions can help much larger communities of amateur athletes achieve their fitness goals. Value-added sponsorships from technology companies like Intel and Samsung can accelerate these benefits when sponsors design custom components.

The worldwide community of 2 billion amateur athletes and fitness practitioners also benefits from the psychological boost of added confidence in the equipment they use. Olympic pole vaulter Jeff Hartwig explained this factor in an interview on "The Tech Race," emphasizing the importance of athletes' confidence in their equipment. In addition to reliability, the durability, accuracy, and energy efficiency of innovations initially developed for Olympic competitions have greater benefits as technologies are transferred to larger markets.

Select technologies initially developed for much larger commercial or military applications are also being adapted for niche applications in sports. GPS mobile location trackers that optimize logistics for fleets and guide drivers to their destinations can also track the speed, movements, and interactions of athletes playing together in team sports, as well as horses selected for equestrian competitions.

Healthy Trends

Carbon fiber prosthetics and wearable airbag injury prevention technologies first developed for use in Olympic sports illustrate a much broader and much more transformative trend. That is the convergence of sports science with health science and the integration of applied sports science with the health care and wellness industries. Research universities such as the University of Ghent in Belgium and Keio University in Japan have already integrated sports and related research into their medical school programs.

The intersection of the sports field with the health care and injury prevention markets offers significant potential based on market size—estimated at $3.6 trillion to $4 trillion by market research experts. But sports technologies have another advantage. They can be commercialized and made available for health care applications much faster than many pharmaceuticals which require clinical trials. And sports technology has not been constrained by the natural phenomenon of antibiotic resistance.

The sports entrepreneurship community is strengthening technology transfer to health care with practical applications. Many can share benefits of Olympic sports expertise with millions of people. Weight management expertise has become important for preventing diabetes. Regular exercise improves bone density and reduces the risk of fractures or chronic conditions that weaken bones. The conditioning of athletic training has demonstrated valuable health benefits.

Olympic athletes such as Anastasia Liukin who put sports experience to work in coaching and training programs designed for mass participation are helping to make the health benefits of sports accessible and affordable. Two good examples are swimmers Kirsty Coventry, who established a nonprofit foundation to manage a swimming academy, and Michael Phelps, who invested in the private swimming academy where he trained himself. Phelps supported its expansion to reach 1,500 new students each year.

Promoting mass participation in sports is just one facet of the contribution the sports community can make to the goal of promoting good health. Many innovative sports-focused ventures are commercializing technologies which have measurable potential to improve the quality of health care and reduce its cost:

- Senaptec, based at the Stadia Ventures incubator, manufactures sophisticated eyewear with a wireless Bluetooth interface. It transmits details of visual performance for analysis and coaching recommendations. Dozens of sports organizations have already integrated Senaptec in their training programs. The start-up's proprietary technology has secured several patents which are facilitating its expansion into the vision care and health care markets.

- Nix Biosensors, another Stadia Ventures backed enterprise, has crafted ultrathin nanotechnology materials to create a prototype patch with sensors that analyze an athlete's sweat during competitions. Designed for endurance sports competitors, the technology analyzes results to recommend timing and source of the best possible hydration choices.

- Fitto is taking a different approach to sports nutrition by customizing pods for athlete clients and programming consumption containers to monitor the progress of sports nutrition programs. The company's incubation at the LeAD sports business incubator is giving it a base in the sports community. Successful proof of concept and endorsements from successful athletes could fast track growth in the much larger health care market of dietary supplements.

- KYMIRA Sport of the United Kingdom has developed athletic clothing using infrared technology to recycle body heat and use it to improve circulation and reduce inflammation. The clothing's demonstrated success in treating pain without medication and accelerating the recovery of fatigued bodies could extend to physical rehabilitation and health care.

- Révèle, launched at the business incubator of the HEC Business School near Paris, has introduced protective gear designed for women competing in combat sports. The firm's proprietary technology gives fabrics shock absorption properties that demonstrate good potential for other injury reduction applications.

Visionary sports entrepreneurs have also transformed mass participation sports events into high-growth profitable businesses. These also encourage sports training's health benefits. Competitor Group of San Diego manages marathon and triathlon races for many communities as a turnkey solution. Gran Fondo Giro d'Italia organizes mass participation group cycle tours for amateurs in scenic locations. World Triathlon Corporation of Tampa, Florida, operates the worldwide IRONMAN triathlon series and has shown how this business model can succeed.

Founded in 1990, IRONMAN expanded globally and encouraged triathletes to participate multiple times with a cumulative point system. The company added related competitions and linked them to its flagship races by also awarding race points. World Triathlon's IRONMAN series charges hefty participation fees. Registration for the 2018 World Championship cost $950. Some regional events cost $200 less, but registrations still sell out frequently. Athletes pay all their own costs for training, travel, and equipment, typically several thousand dollars. This is notably different than the Olympics, which covers all costs of athlete participation during the Olympic Games and provides Olympic Solidarity athletic scholarships. IRONMAN athletes must pay an annual registration fee and their membership provides sponsors frequent marketing opportunities. Sponsors also pay to sell directly to athletes and spectators on site.

The financial results of World Triathlon Corporation have been excellent and strengthened prospects for other sports business seeking investments. Revenues and net profits have grown 40 percent annually. The company's founders invested $3 million in 1990 and financed expansion by reinvesting profits in the business. By 2008, it was worth $85 million when private investors at Providence Equity Securities purchased the company. Seven years later, Dalian Wanda Group of China paid total consideration estimated at $650 million.

World Triathlon is a private, for-profit company separate from the Olympics. Triathlon's status as an Olympic sport has been advantageous, supporting sophisticated training by coaches and athletes and a critical mass of participation that helps to make development of customized triathlon products more profitable. Most recent Olympic medalists in men's triathlon have also been IRONMAN champions, illustrating another way the Olympics' approach to cooperating with private ventures is stimulating growth across the sports industry.

The Olympic Ecosystem Gives Sports Entrepreneurs a Competitive Edge

Lausanne, headquarters of the International Olympic Committee and most international sports federations, is adding momentum and credibility to the sports entrepreneurship surge. In 2016, the region's sports community started an innovation network dubbed "ThinkSport" to connect the region's talent pool. Two years later, it launched a new sports business incubator to put the talent pool to work and added an international sports business start-up venture contest.

The ThinkSport new venture contest provided up-to-date insights about success factors for sports start-ups. It also highlighted important differences of the sports industry that successful start-ups will need to manage. Two of the judges in the initial selection round were international sports federation executives. ISF's roles in setting uniform standards and selecting official suppliers for international competitions makes their evaluation of future business potential an important factor for many investors.

ThinkSport welcomed international entrants from other countries, following the global sourcing approach already in place at Stadia Ventures, Courtside Ventures, and the LeAD business incubator. These pioneers seek opportunities created by the global talent pool that the sports world has built.

The ThinkSport 2018 sports venture contest winners showed how sports can create niche markets in which entrepreneurial businesses can thrive:

- Grand prize winner ForwardGame, based at the LeAD business incubator, has leveraged the popularity of electronic games developed for mobile phones to integrate an e-sports format with physical sports activities and simplify scorekeeping.
- Fanpictor is using smartphones to customize an offering for the sports market. Its proprietary technology makes a spectator's smartphone an extension of the audio-visual system operated in a sports stadium.

- SportDiet is adapting smartphones and connected devices to make sports nutrition know-how from high-performance sports institutes accessible to everyday athletes.

Unlike smartphone-focused sports start-ups, ThinkSport 2018 contest finalist Resero is building a business opportunity based on the undependability of smartphones in rigorous outdoor sports environments. The Resero Whistle utilizes a mesh of communications networks and GPS technology to pinpoint the exact location of an athlete endangered by emergency conditions to send an alert for a quick rescue. With the number of sports related emergencies reaching one-half million annually, demand for this type of technology application is significant.

Collectively, the entrepreneurial start-ups that are winning attention in the sports world are showing that the scale of market opportunities related to sports is large. This, in turn, is motivating higher levels of innovation and investment, strengthening the infrastructure for the sports industry to grow in the future. Successful sports start-ups reinforce confidence that entrepreneurial sports businesses can leverage the talent pool and networks that connect the world of high-performance sports.

The sports talent pool supports teamwork with International Sports Federations and National Olympic Committees. This strength was featured by many presenters at the ThinkSport new venture contest. Several have focused their product development on specific needs of sports federations:

- Wiz Team provides software solutions for managing details of sports events so that smaller scale events can emulate Olympic test events.
- My Next Match has developed an electronic medical passport program for athletes participating in international competitions to simplify the tasks sports federations need to complete to manage athlete health and safety.
- Proskida of Canada has developed sensors and data analysis programs adopted by the Canadian, Swiss, and Norwegian Olympic cross-country skiing teams.

Successful collaboration with international sports federations often appeals to investors in early-stage companies who seek stable sources of future revenues and a competitive edge from the federations' exclusive rights to organize Olympic qualifying events. Most sports federations register thousands of athletes and supporters and control event calendars that effectively guarantee steady cash flows for years into the future. The federations have also established partnerships with equipment suppliers and equipment testing institutions, making them dependable partners for quality control.

The collaborative style of sports start-ups lowers costs at incubators and co-working spaces. It is a natural progression from shared training facilities in an Olympic Village. And the collaborative style that stands out in these sports facilities also attracts potential investors. Privately owned professional sports teams are a significant source of expansion capital and bankable contracts in the sports world. The large diversified suppliers of sports gear and equipment also regularly acquire successful sports start-ups.

While both sports start-ups and sports incubators promote the competitive advantages of teamwork, popular sports references such as "home run" or "hole-in-one" are rare. The entrepreneurial community in the sports world attracts highly competitive players. But sports traditions and team spirit, as well as the important role of not-for-profit sports organizations, encourage more collaborative management compared to some other areas of venture investing. Many proponents of the Olympics' promotion of entrepreneurship call this "social entrepreneurship."

A prominent early-stage investor in entrepreneurial start-ups sees how the approach of many sports start-ups could open doors for financing from investors who are actively looking elsewhere. In 2017, Ray Chan, managing partner of the ACE Fund, told fellow investors at the Tech Coast Angels syndicate:

> Entrepreneurs and private investors in flyover states (areas not located on the two coasts of the USA) don't have the need—or the huge pressure—to have to hit a home run…they are satisfied with a base hit. And that means quicker exits for angel investors.

A year later, groups of California based investors took Chan's advice and traveled to Switzerland to screen prospects at the ThinkSport venture program and other accelerators.

IOC leaders found so much potential in sports entrepreneurship that they launched a new sports business accelerator designed for the Olympic Community in October 2018. It is called the "Athlete365 Business Accelerator." All former Olympic athletes will be eligible to participate in introductory training. The most promising project proposals will receive additional support adequate to complete working prototypes and make sophisticated investor presentations.

A Case in Point: Advanced Sport Instruments

Eight-time Academy Award winner Edith Head is well remembered for her famous quote, "You can have anything you want in life if you dress for it." Sports is taking this aspiration to the next level with sophisticated wearable devices that measure key metrics of athlete performance and analyze results to pinpoint the choices most likely to succeed. Advanced Sport Instruments (ASI), based in Lausanne, Switzerland, is capitalizing on this opportunity by designing and marketing a 35-gram precision measurement device integrated in lightweight vests for athletes.

Wearable electronic performance and tracking systems have helped sports teams to improve so much that FIFA adopted rule changes and policies to set uniform standards for their use by teams training for international competitions. The federation also prohibited use for transmission to technical staff during FIFA matches to promote its vision of fairness. ASI was one of several suppliers which received approval for the FIFA International Match Standard. This gave the young company, founded in 2011, a competitive advantage and good reference.

Looking forward, the company recognized the need to capitalize on as many advantages as possible to stay ahead of competitors in its market. It leveraged the support available from local business promotion organizations in Lausanne, obtaining business coaching from Innovaud and exhibiting at a sports technology convention and investment presentation event put together by ThinkSport, the Lausanne based sports business industry association. Switzerland Global Enterprise also gave ASI the opportunity to exhibit at the 2019 Consumer Electronics Show in Las Vegas, the world's largest marketplace for all things electronic.

ASI worked to maximize the functionality of its technology solution so that it would appeal to both sports teams and Value Added Resellers who signed up to represent ASI products in 30 countries. FieldWiz, the ASI sensor, integrates measurement of player motion and heart rate and applies sophisticated software to improve the ability of coaches and players to optimize performance. This approach supports uniform, objective analysis to measure the results of game plans and training regimens. The uniformity has an additional advantage for national teams competing in Olympic qualifying events, which frequently rely on athletes who play for different professional teams during the rest of the season.

ASI will have to build its own team to make the most of its opportunities. The company had nine employees at the start of 2019. It planned to add 10 or more in the following year. The ASI team will continue to develop and market the company's products, which are engineered in Switzerland and manufactured to specification by an affiliated precision technology vendor.

After exhibiting at the 2019 Consumer Electronics Show in Las Vegas, ASI recruited a new business development manager for the U.S. market. The plan to grow sales in the United States foresees additional distribution partners and Value Added Resellers targeting new clients in team sports including soccer, American football, rugby, ice hockey, and basketball.

ASI's global growth plan requires specialized sports industry expertise. The company is focused on two large international sports sectors—outdoor team sports played in stadiums such as football and rugby, plus outdoor winter sports competitions in Olympic disciplines. The experience of the Swiss ski team in training with ASI solutions before the 2018 Winter Olympic Games provided a good reference.

This focus is helping ASI achieve its goal of providing a cost-effective technology solution to quickly build its customer base. The base price for a docking station including 10 sensors is 4,499 Euros, within the budget of almost every team in its target markets. By the start of 2019, ASI's measurement devices were used by over 500 teams and more than 6,000 sets had been sold.

The young company's sales success and technical certification by FIFA impressed local investors. In 2018, ASI raised CHF 355,000 in equity from a group of angel investors affiliated with the Business Angels Switzerland group and secured a CHF 300,000 loan from the Foundation for Technological Innovation.

ASI founder and CEO Lionel Yersin encourages other entrepreneurial businesses in sports to follow this approach. His advice is simple: "Always keep one goal in mind and stay focused."

Illustration 3.1 Sports technology start-up ASI (right) is setting a fast pace in the application of wearable electronic devices to analyze athlete performance, and Enmouvement is showing how innovative start-ups can accelerate the convergence of sports and health care.

Key Sources and References

Athlete 365 Newsroom. March 9, 2017. "A Record Year for the IOC Athlete Learning Gateway." Published Online: https://olympic.org/athlete365/news/a-record-year-for-the-ioc-athlete-learning-gateway-and-more-to-come-in-2017/

Badenhausen, K. 2012. "Why ESPN Is Worth $40 Billion as the World's Most Valuable Media Property." *Forbes.com*, November 9.

Frater, P. 2015. "China's Wanda Completes $650 Million World Triathlon Buy." *Variety*, August 26.

Hays, G. July 24, 2019. "Kerri Walsh Jennings Looks to Shape Beach Volleyball's Future with New p1440 Partnership." *ESPNW.com*.

Jans, G. February 5, 2017. "Bode Miller: Aztech Mountain statt Ski-Comeback." *ISPO.com*. Published online: https://ispo.com/people/id_79699214/us-skistar-bode-miller-begraebt-comeback-plaene.html

Olympic Channel. 2018. "The Tech Race" *(Television Series)*. Published online: https://olympicchannel.com/en/original-series/detail/the-tech-race/

Owen, D. November 14, 2005. "Fred Perry's surprise big hit." Published online: https://ft.com/content/a7cbd23c-5538-11da-8a74-00000e25118c

Pfeffer, T.J. February 22, 2018. "The History of the MIT Sloan Sports Analytics Conference." *MetroMBA*. Published online: https://metromba.com/2018/02/history-mit-sloan-sports-analytics/

Ristiyana, A., H.S. Maryo., P.V.H. Trang., and Z. Setiawan. April 1, 2012. "Strategic Brand Management: Lacoste." Published online: https://brandlacoste.wordpress.com/

Sato, K. 2015. "Billionaire Explains Why Sports Investments Have Skyrocketed." *Inc. Magazine*, May 7.

Scott, A. February 13, 2014. "TechnoGym Founder Builds an Empire of Health and Fitness." *The National UAE*. Published online: https://thenational.ae/business/technogym-founder-builds-an-empire-of-health-and-fitness-1.574272

United States Sports Academy Course List SAM 662 Sports Entrepreneurship. Published online: https://ussa.edu/academics/doctorate-sports-management/courses/

Weiner, Y. December 18, 2017. "29 Pro Athletes Who Became Entrepreneurs, And How They Are Still Winning Out Of The Stadium." Published online: https://medium.com/thrive-global/29-pro-athletes-who-became-entrepreneurs-and-how-they-are-still-winning-out-of-the-stadium-dfef5e06c9bf

CHAPTER 4

Jumping Hurdles

A Tale of Two Stadiums

The official press release reporting the financial results of the London 2012 organizing committee showed achievement of a balanced budget. This is a standard goal of well managed not-for-profit enterprises. The reported operating revenues of UKL 2.41 billion and expenditures of UKL 2.38 billion met this goal and budget estimates of London 2012 organizers.

Six years after a picture-perfect London 2012 Summer Olympics, the auditing firm Ernst & Young published a financial report with a different perspective. This detailed the financial results of E20 Stadium, the owner and operator of Queen Elizabeth II Park, which had served as the main venue for the London 2012 Games. The report showed an operating loss of UKL 268 million (about $350 million) in 2017 and contained the financial reporting equivalent of "out of bounds" in the sporting world: "*The Stadium fair value at 31 March 2018 is held at nil due to the partnership's financial forecast.*"

Future forecasts predicted the worst was over, but far from the Olympic value of excellence. Management projected additional operating losses of UKL 100 million (about $135 million) over the next five years. Eighty-two percent of the losses were expected to be covered by taxpayer funded enterprises which own the London Legacy Development Corporation, owner of E20 Stadium. The UKL 20 million grant distributed by London 2012 after the Games and future fundraising would be needed to cover other operating losses.

The privately owned and operated O2 Arena located five miles south of Queen Elizabeth II Park had much, much better results to report. The 2017 operating revenues were UKL 97 million and net profits an astonishing UKL 33.5 million. The net profit margin of 34 percent ranked it among the most profitable business operations in the world. Apple, Inc., whose market value had exceeded $1 trillion, has achieved impressive net profit margins of 28 percent, but is a silver medalist compared to London's O2 Arena.

O2 Arena rented its facilities to London 2012 for basketball and gymnastics competitions. Its 2012 net profit margin of 25 percent put it in the top tier of well managed private companies and helped to finance a London 2012 sponsorship.

The financial success of the O2 Arena during 2012 and after the Games can boost the optimism of Olympics advocates. AEG, an American company which owns and manages London's O2 Arena, manages 150 other sports and event venues in the United States and a dozen foreign countries. It has also been a longstanding supporter of the Los Angeles 2028 Olympics organization. Of the 19 venues planned to present the 2028 Summer Olympics in Los Angeles, 4 are managed by AEG, which also manages arenas in Beijing and Paris, the 2022 and 2024 Olympics host cites.

A closer look at the advantages AEG has built to outperform government owned facilities can help the Olympics move past earlier challenges with facilities plans. This could win support from cities and countries that consider hosting future Olympics. From a business perspective, AEG has established a "distinctive competence" in the management of sports and event facilities and gained additional advantages from "best of class" status. This model should be familiar to the leaders of the Olympics. It is similar to the approach the Olympics has used to produce international multisport competitions and excellent television programming.

Higher, Higher, Higher

Many things have changed during the history of the Olympics, but frequently the costs of hosting the Olympics have moved higher, higher, higher. London carried out the 1948 Olympics as the "Austerity Olympics," a stark contrast to the extravagance of Berlin in 1936. Since then, many Olympic hosts have opted to impress international visitors and television viewers with elaborate ceremonies and building projects. These became major obligations as the practice of awarding the Olympics through competitive bidding took hold.

In 2016, the Said Business School at Oxford University published a rigorous look at Olympics host city expenditures over time, including inflation adjustments. Detailed figures are not available for five Olympics from 1964 to 2016 and the scale of both Winter and Summer Olympics more than doubled over five decades. But the trend was clear. The final report showed that the average inflation adjusted operating expenditures for the Summer Olympics had grown from $282 million in Tokyo in 1964 to reach $5.2 billion.

The increase in operating costs for the Winter Olympics was steeper. Innsbruck, Austria, reported operating costs of $22 million to present the 1964 Winter Olympics. Fifty years later, the accounting for the Sochi 2014 Winter Olympics reported $22 billion, a 1,000-fold increase! This figure may be impressive to some, but it is intimidating to others, and influenced voters in a long list of cities which decided not to host the 2022 or 2026 Winter Olympics—Munich, St. Moritz, Sion, Graz, and Calgary.

Economists often refer to a figure such as the $22 billion for Sochi 2014 as an "outlier." It is 10 times higher than the median for 12 previous Olympic Winter Games for which figures are available. But all Olympic Games in the 21st century have been multibillion dollar productions.

From a global perspective, multibillion dollar investments promoting Olympic sports have paid good dividends. Following the 2014 Winter Olympics, market research firm A.T. Kearney published a comprehensive study of the global sports economy. The results included a conservative estimate of worldwide annual revenues in sports and fitness at $650 billion. This figure does not include related sports travel, which United Airlines reports as the second largest leisure category. Total global spending on leisure travel was estimated at $7 trillion in 2014.

The outlook for 2020 is impressive. As the sports industry continues to outpace world economic growth, sports industry revenues should cross the $800 billion mark in 2020. Professional sports is highly visible with media coverage and spectators, but only accounts for about 13 percent of the total. Participant sports such as marathons and the IRONMAN triathlon series, generates revenues 30 percent greater than professional sports, driven by the very large base of 2 billion participants worldwide. Capital spending on infrastructure from stadiums to golf courses to tennis courts and soccer fields, plus related software and services, adds up to over $200 billion a year. Experts acknowledge the difficulties of calculating a precise figure, since many facilities such as Wembley Stadium are used for concerts and other events. The sporting goods equipment category is projected to reach $400 billion worldwide in 2020, based on historic growth rates.

These impressive figures do not include sports spending at public schools and programs sponsored by charities. Average spending of $500 per participant adds up. The combined secondary school enrollment of Canada, Mexico, and the United States is 18.5 million, so estimates for total school spending on sports for the three countries exceed $9 billion.

China is planning to greatly increase the global sports industry's scale. One long-term objective of hosting the 2022 Winter Olympics in Beijing is to expand Chinese participation in winter sports to 300 million in the next generation. China's plan for growth in sports equipment and services is also ambitious, targeting $800 billion in revenue in 2025. If this growth occurs, global sports revenues will approach $2 trillion in the next decade and sports industry sales will surpass the pharmaceuticals industry.

Spending on sports has had a beneficial impact on employment. According to U.S. Bureau of Labor Statistics data, six and a half full-time equivalent jobs are created to support each professional athlete. The average annual compensation for these jobs in the United States is $41,200. That is less than half of what most professional athletes earn, but the over 120,000 jobs created boost economic prosperity.

As global competition and recruiting have become common in sports, these U.S. benchmarks now reflect global trends—and show that the Olympics' goal of encouraging participation in sports is a significant driver of economic growth. Professional sports and organized amateur sports employ over a quarter million workers in the United States alone and over 1 million worldwide. Service providers in medicine, law, accounting, and other professions, create more employment.

As voters in 10 prospective Olympic host cities showed, the benefit of global economic growth is often not a persuasive argument for local governments to fund the multibillion dollar costs of hosting an Olympics. To date, the Olympics has jumped over this difficult hurdle and concluded workable host city contracts. In the long term, alternative approaches to paying for the Olympics will have to get more attention.

The list of candidate cities where city officials or voters decided against hosting the Olympics is long. Boston, Rome, Hamburg, and Budapest withdrew bids for the 2024 Summer Olympic Games. Voters in Munich, St. Moritz, Sion, Graz, and Calgary decided against bids for the 2022 or 2026 Winter Olympic Games. Oslo withdrew its bid for 2022. The cities which agreed to host the Olympics in 2022, 2024, 2026, and 2028—Beijing, Paris, Milan, and Los Angeles, respectively—succeeded in gaining the backing of city officials but did not hold elections.

Following voters' defeat of the proposal to host the 2026 Winter Olympic Games in Calgary, Professor Michael Heine of the Olympic Studies Center of Western University in Ontario, Canada, discussed the key issues in an interview with *Bloomberg News*:

- Olympic host cities have not had net economic and financial benefits relative to costs.
- Initial bid cost figures are low compared to actual expenditures in all cases.
- The scale of the Olympics makes it challenging even for large cities like London and Beijing to host the Olympic Games.
- It has become necessary to assume that scandals have tarnished the Olympic brand.

Heine also acknowledged the IOC's efforts to address these challenges by reducing the costs of submitting a bid and using existing facilities. He observed that so far Pyeongchang 2018 and Tokyo 2020 had not reported substantial benefits, while actual total expenditures exceeded estimates.

The cost/benefit equation for official host cities has challenged some of the traditional approaches to organizing and financing the Games. In 2010, 2012, and 2016, the private enterprises responsible for converting housing at the official Olympic Athlete's Villages to privately owned residences could not complete the task. This required additional taxpayer financing until the properties were ultimately sold. Property prices in Vancouver and London increased, so covering the additional expenses with additional income from property taxes provided a solution.

Taxpayer opposition in Olympic host cities is nothing new. In 1934, renowned musical composer Richard Wagner wrote to the town council of Garmisch-Partenkirchen objecting strongly to any use of local tax money for the 1936 Winter Olympic Games. Wagner was ultimately persuaded to support the Games with a commission to compose a new overture for the opening of the 1936 Summer Olympic Games in Berlin.

Olympic bid opponents often raise concerns about future burdens to taxpayers. But widespread government deficits expand that burden to nearly everyone, not just taxpayers, and shift responsibility for paying government debts to younger people. In Japan, host country of the 2020 Summer Olympic Games, the national debt as a percentage of gross domestic product surpassed the threshold of 250 percent for the first time in 2018. These economic realities are not easy to reconcile with traditional Olympic values and their emphasis on youth. Political opponents of the Olympics portray this as "three weeks of party and thirty years of debt."

The 2016 Oxford Said School of Business study of Olympic hosting costs cited specific reasons for the history of final costs greatly exceeding original projections at Olympic Games since 1964. The fixed completion deadlines limit local organizing committee flexibility and can necessitate overtime costs and express deliveries. Cost estimates based on past projects without such rigorous deadlines were not directly comparable.

The scale of Olympic Games cost overruns is large by any standard. The 2016 Oxford Said School of Business study cited median cost overruns of 83 percent in Summer Olympic Games since 1964 and 118 percent in the Winter Games over the same period.

A 2017 report by Mari Yamaguchi of Associated Press identified two recurring factors in the excess of actual expenditures over original bid figures. First, initial bids submitted to the IOC just include the estimated costs of facilities and programs that are required by the IOC and exclude related expenditures for security, transit infrastructure, and additional public services desired for the Games. Second, Olympic bids have consistently used the lowest cost estimate for each individual component. However, when plans are implemented, some low bidders may not be able to work with other contractors or obtain bank financing for their proposals.

Many successful private businesses have not had this type of financial management difficulty. The stark contrast between London's Olympic Stadium being formally declared worthless while a similar facility located nearby produces exceptional profits year after year should provide a lesson which Olympic leaders will want to learn. The recent history of the Olympics has already encouraged serious thought and some action in this direction.

Health and Human Performance

The Olympics has been an influential thought leader in promoting physical fitness and wellness as foundations for good health. Medical schools, clinics, public health agencies, and several insurance firms have strengthened this development.

The upside that the health and human performance sector can add to Olympic programs is substantial. At the time of the 2018 Winter Olympics, high end estimates of global sports industry size were in the $700 billion range. By contrast, the Global Wellness Institute reports the size of the global wellness sector, including health foods and therapeutic fitness programs, at five times the sports industry alone.

Tokyo 2020 is adding momentum to this trend. International Gymnastics Federation President Morinari Watanabe, a member of the IOC and the Tokyo 2020 Executive Committee, highlighted the potential for sports to re-energize aging societies as the keynote speaker of the 2017 "Sport for Tomorrow" program in Japan. His ambitious call to action was "I want all of you to do your best to become the kind of innovators who will make it possible for people to say 100 or 200 years from now that it was sports that saved our society from the ongoing aging of the population."

Prominent medical research leaders are seconding the motion. They have joined together to share research and implementation practices in a forum called the "Academic Consortium for Integrative Medicine and Health." Nine of the top 10 medical schools in the United States, 5 Canadian medical schools, and the U.S. Veterans Administration participate together with 55 other medical research programs. The emphasis on health and human performance focuses significant attention on sports and physical activity as treatments for patients with diabetes, cancer, and other common ailments, as well as strategies for containing the worldwide obesity crisis. Yoga and other fitness regimens receive serious attention. But Olympic sports are fundamental.

Duke University has established a dedicated institute for wellness called Duke Integrative Medicine. It employs the coaching model pioneered by the sports world to prepare professionals for assignments in health and human performance. Duke's online training resources are encouraging widespread participation.

The School of Medicine at Stanford University, a founding member of the consortium, is showing how health and human performance initiatives can benefit excellence in sports. It has built a human performance laboratory supporting all 900 varsity athletes at Stanford and produces research helping other medical schools to advance sports science. Its official mission is ambitious: "interdisciplinary research integrating fields of biomechanics, biomedical engineering, physiology and exercise physiology, orthopedics, mechanobiology, and exercise rehabilitation."

The Stanford Medical School human performance lab provides a close-up of sports science in action. It is equipped with instruments which can measure key heart, lung, muscle, bone, and joint strength metrics in varying conditions for athletes performing any sport. This data can be used to optimize preparations, performance, and recovery. Coaches can also use the data to select and rotate athletes for better results.

The Stanford human performance lab also developed a sophisticated program customized for endurance and ultra-endurance athletes. It calculated precise measurements of cardiovascular fitness and aerobic endurance to recommend exercise and nutrition regimens to improve performance and stamina.

While the Stanford Medical School human performance lab is focused on high-performance sports, advanced research there is producing greater benefits. Its treatments for injury prevention and illness prevention, together with health and wellness regimens, are reaching the general public.

No other program can match Stanford's 23 consecutive years ranking first place among U.S. college sports programs. Not surprisingly, the expenses are substantial. In the 2017–2018 academic year, Stanford's undergraduate college spent $9,660 per student on sports education and facilities. That is equivalent to $75,000 for each varsity athlete. The University of Southern California, the only university with more Olympic athlete alumni than Stanford, spends even more—$94,000 per varsity athlete.

The Olympic solidarity athletic scholarship program also allocates substantial resources to match the high costs of training high-performance athletes. In 2016, the average grant per athlete was $83,400, a figure competitive with Stanford and the University of Southern California. The infrastructure for high-performance training centers and widespread knowledge sharing are expanding the benefits of both athletic training and injury prevention expertise from these kinds of programs. In 2019, the Association of Sports Performance Centres organized its global conference with the private Barca Sports Innovation Hub, accelerating key knowledge sharing with the sports world.

The cumulative investment in the 88 high-performance sports facilities closely affiliated with the Olympics and the IOC Athletes Commission makes this network an influential force in health and human performance. Infrastructure investments in these types of facilities range from $7 million for the smallest regional facility in Australia to just over $1 billion for the Singapore Sports Institute. The Barcelona area facility alone invested 36 million Euro in 2010 (about $50 million at the time). These sums are impressive compared to the $25 million average investment by professional venture capital firms in health care enterprises. The collective infrastructure represents over $4.5 billion in assets focused on facilitating high-performance sports. These investments are significant on their own, but the value of infrastructure investments made in Olympic-affiliated high-performance sports training facilities was similar to the total book value of assets of independent health care technology companies listed on the NASDAQ stock exchange in 2018.

According to Fidelity Investments, at the end of 2018 independent health care technology companies reported an average share price multiple of 75 times earnings. That was much higher than the average of 20 times earnings reported for the S+P 500 Index, a benchmark used widely for all industries collectively. This shows that the financial community expects very high value added from this sector for many years into the future.

A driver of high valuations for both the health care technology sector and high-performance sports science sector is the challenge that antibiotic resistance is presenting to the traditional health care industry. A March 2018 conference on antibiotic resistance at the Pasteur Institute presented eight case studies of infections that had become more difficult to treat with conventional antibiotics, including tuberculosis and salmonella. Medical experts also documented the evolution of multiresistant bacteria which could not be reliably treated with combination therapies, commonly called "super-bugs." Discovering new medical treatments might address some of these challenges, but the years needed for clinical testing and regulatory approval make this a slow solution. Systematically promoting good health and strong immune systems through physical fitness stands out as an essential approach to this global health challenge.

Worldwide efforts to promote health and human performance and partner with the business community are redefining the modern Olympics. When a group of educators launched the modern Olympics at the Sorbonne University in 1894, the program was part of the physical education field. After 125 years, many sports organizations are incorporating health and human performance to stay competitive. An overview of sports management programs which are managed by health and human performance departments illuminates this trend:

- American Public University Department of Health and Sport Studies, West Virginia
- The Citadel Health and Human Performance Department, South Carolina
- Concordia University Nebraska Health and Human Performance Studies, Nebraska
- Keio University Graduate School of Health Management, Fujisawa, Japan
- Nippon Sport Science University Faculty of Health and Sport Science, Yokohama, Japan
- Oregon State University College of Public Health, Oregon
- Rutgers University Department of Kinesiology and Health, New Jersey
- Southern Methodist University Department of Applied Physiology and Wellness, Texas
- Syracuse University Falk College of Sport and Human Dynamics, New York
- Teikyo University Faculty of Medical Technology, Tokyo, Japan

- Tennessee State University College of Health Sciences, Tennessee
- University of Bologna Wellness and Sport Management Faculty, Bologna, Italy
- University of Ghent School of Medicine, Ghent, Belgium
- University of Florida College of Health and Human Performance, Florida
- University of Indianapolis College of Health Sciences, Indiana
- University of Western States Sports Medicine Program, Oregon

The University of Ghent Medical School's Victoris program illustrates how sports science based on health and human performance expertise can promote sports and fitness activities and engage the Olympic community. The program connects external business and sports organizations with relevant research to accelerate practical applications and adaptation of new technology. Projects focused on injury prevention, physical rehabilitation, and nutrition bridge traditional approaches to health care management and new practices. Digital technologies designed to manage and expand sports and fitness activities reinforce traditional goals of the Olympic community.

The University of Ghent has particularly close connections to Olympic sports. Dr. Jacques Rogge, who served as IOC president from 2001 to 2013, is a graduate of the medical school and championed the founding of the sports science laboratory there. Rogge advocated the policy of "sport for all" during his tenure as IOC president. He helped expand infrastructure and financing for greater sports participation, as well as more sports demonstrations by Olympic athletes.

Olympic community leaders are promoting connections between sports and the broader field of health and human performance. This is an important theme on its own. But vocal opposition to hosting the Olympics expressed in a dozen prospective host cities is making an emphasis on health and performance a strategy to win support for future Olympics. The IOC is highlighting research from a partner institution, the "Active Well Being Initiative," to build support, reminding the public that:

- Treatment of physical inactivity and related chronic disease conditions costs $54 billion each year worldwide.
- The estimated level of preventable deaths from chronic diseases which could be avoided by adequate physical fitness is 1.6 million worldwide every year.
- Obesity levels more than doubled between 1980 and 2014.

The physical fitness and public health professions now recognize the scale of the obesity epidemic and the need for physical fitness programs to help reduce health risks. In 2015, the American College of Cardiology published the results of the first extensive long-term study of health deterioration linked to the obesity epidemic. The study found that 51.5 percent of a group diagnosed as obese developed serious and potentially fatal health problems over a 20-year period; only 10.6 percent of a group of healthy normal weight individuals with similar demographics developed serious health problems over the same period. The study documented a crisis that public health and insurance professionals confront daily—obese individuals become seriously ill five times more often than persons maintaining a weight range normal for their size.

Health and Superhuman Performance

It is not possible and not helpful to overlook the significant difference between the physical fitness ideals envisioned by the modern Olympics' founders and the scale of more recent performance enhancing treatment abuse, widely referred to as doping. So many cases took so long to detect, the public may never know the full scale of abuse.

This Olympic sized problem has a long history. Cheating was not unheard of at the ancient Olympics. Athletes found violating its strict rules were obliged to pay monetary fines and install statues called Zanes. There were hundreds in the 1,168 year history of the ancient Olympics.

The details of the large and systematic doping program conducted in East Germany under Communist leadership show how extensive athlete doping can be and how difficult it can be to uncover. Two civil cases conducted after the Communist period revealed the former East German doping program's scope and scale. Over 100,000 young athletes, that is

2 percent of East Germans born between 1950 and 1970, were directed to take Turinabol pills by East German coaches. This program was state funded and state directed, as documents made public later ultimately proved.

Credible reports in foreign newspapers had raised suspicions about the East German sports doping program shortly after it began. In September 1973, *France Soir* published a feature asserting that women athletes in East Germany, then called the German Democratic Republic (GDR), were being injected with male hormones. The report also claimed that both male and female athletes were given anabolic steroids in pill form. Archived GDR documents later proved these reports were true.

The long-term health consequences for many former athletes were serious. Hormonal imbalances, infertility, miscarriages, and birth defects were common maladies. The two cases conducted on behalf of the athletes concluded with payments of about 10,000 Euros ($12,000) for each athlete.

The Olympic community has not been able to do much about this massive manipulation of competition. The 541 Olympic medals won by former East German athletes were not reallocated to the competitors from other countries who ranked below them. German courts tried coaches and doctors who directed the doping program; they were found guilty, but the resulting suspended sentences did not support the Olympic values of respect and fair play. The World Anti-Doping Agency (WADA) was not started until 1999.

Since WADA was founded, it has had a heavy workload. The effort to detect and eliminate abuse of performance enhancing treatments has been characterized as an arms race in which antidoping executives face continuing challenges to uncover new and often devious ways to transform human performance into synthetic performance. In addition, recruiting well-trained medical professionals and technical support staff for testing facilities can be difficult or prohibitively expensive.

London 2012 organizers spent UKL 20 million ($28 million) for a state-of-the-art drug testing laboratory and also paid for over 1,000 temporary staff. Planned capacity was to test 6,250 athletes, 60 percent of those competing. The plan included tests for all medalists and storing blood samples for retesting using more sophisticated technologies when these became available. Seven years later, reanalysis of stored samples detected 116 cases of doping code violations, primarily anabolic steroids.

The frequency with which sophisticated, expensive athlete sample testing facilities have been out of service has underscored a large management challenge:

- In 2015, Russia's drug testing and reporting facilities were decertified by the WADA. Russia's accreditation was subsequently revoked entirely and not reinstated until September 2018 with outside inspections required. In addition, the Olympic committees of Andorra, Argentina, Israel, Kenya, Ukraine, and Bolivia were found noncompliant with testing and reporting procedures and were also sanctioned.

- In 2016, WADA decertified China's only drug testing facility from April 22 to August 15, citing inadequate supervision. In the course of the year, the previously accredited laboratories in Almaty, Kazakhstan; Bloemfontein, South Africa; Lisbon, Portugal; Doha, Qatar; Madrid, Spain; and Mexico City were also suspended for months until they could fulfill the most current accreditation criteria. In addition, in late June 2016 the Brazilian sports drug testing facility on site at the Rio 2016 Olympics was found inadequate by the International Standards Organization. Rio's shortcomings were managed in the next four weeks in time for the Summer Games, but the experience weakened confidence.

- In 2017, a series of unsatisfactory inspections resulted in more testing facilities being partially or fully suspended. Accreditations for Almaty, Kazakhstan, and Bloemfontein, South Africa, were revoked entirely. Bogota, Columbia, received a six-month suspension. The UCLA Olympic testing laboratory was partially suspended for four types of tests. France's official athlete drug testing laboratory reported itself as noncompliant following technical difficulties and was suspended by WADA in September and reinstated three months later.

- The year 2018 did not achieve measurable improvement. Sports drug testing laboratories in Bogota, Columbia, and

Bucharest, Romania, were completely suspended for six months and the Stockholm laboratory was partially suspended. Then in October, the Lisbon, Portugal, laboratory previously suspended by WADA for a year in 2016 was suspended again.

In the entire world, there are only 35 permanent comprehensive athlete drug testing facilities fully equipped to carry out analysis suitable for the Olympics and Olympic qualifying events, which were initially approved by WADA. This figure includes a new facility in Nairobi, Kenya, opened in the summer of 2018 and the Russian laboratory reinstated in late 2018, but not compliant with all conditions for complete accreditation. That means *two-fifths* of WADA accredited athlete drug testing facilities did not meet standards set by WADA or the International Standards Organization at least once in the four years following the Sochi 2014 Winter Olympic Games.

Revocation and suspension rates for automobile driver's licenses in the United States make the 40 percent revocation/suspension rates for these elite athlete drug testing facilities look very high. In 2017, only 4 of 50 states had a rate over 5 percent—Nebraska, Indiana, Ohio, and North Dakota, and the national median was under 4 percent. Of course, accreditation of drug testing facilities is more rigorous than automobile driver's license regulation. But this stark contrast helps explain why errors of an elite athlete drug testing facility are not insurable risks, although it is possible to purchase insurance for injuries caused by unlicensed drivers.

The devil is in the details. Most modern commerce depends on insurance to carry on with business as usual. Inventories can be damaged by fires or floods—and there is insurance for that. Foreign exchange rates could change—and there is insurance for that in the form of hedging contracts. Couriers could lose shipments of components or documents—and provide some insurance coverage automatically plus additional coverage at higher rates. But no athlete can obtain insurance for financial losses caused by antidoping code violations by another athlete. It is economically impossible to provide this type of insurance with an historical facility failure rate of 40 percent and retesting results that show an error rate of 2 percent in earlier tests.

Most other risks in the sports world are insurable. For example, World Rugby obtains insurance to compensate owners of professional teams when rugby players are unable to play following injuries at World Rugby international games outside the professional leagues.

There is yet another dimension to this complex challenge. Many athletes who competed at past Olympics without any disciplinary action for doping code violations at the Olympics were charged and disciplined at other sports events. For example,

- Jan Ullrich of Germany won both a gold medal and a silver medal in cycling events at Sydney 2000; he was later disciplined with a two-year ban from cycling in 2012 and confirmed in a 2013 media interview that he had received blood doping treatments from Spanish doctor Eufemiano Fuentes.
- Alexandre Vinokourov of Kazakhstan won a gold medal in the men's cycling road race at the London 2012 Olympics after serving a two-year ban for performance enhancing blood transfusions taken during the 2007 Tour de France.
- Lance Armstrong of the United States, a cycling bronze medalist at Sydney 2000, was later disgraced as a serial abuser of performance enhancing treatments; although he produced some documents asserting his treatments were medically necessary, he was compelled to return his Olympic medal to the U.S. Olympic Committee.
- Justin Gatlin won gold, silver, and bronze medals in athletics at the Athens 2004 Olympics, as well as a bronze medal at London 2012 and a silver medal at Rio 2016. He could not compete at Beijing 2008 because the IAAF had disciplined him with a four-year ban in 2006 for testosterone supplementation.
- Maria Sharapova won a silver medal in tennis at the London 2012 Olympics. In 2016, the International Tennis Union suspended her for 15 months following a positive test for meldonium, a heart medication, at the 2016 Australian Open.

Sharapova's case highlighted the complexity of managing performance enhancement prohibitions. Meldonium was added to the list of prohibited substances effective January 1, 2016, just three weeks before the Australian Open. The e-mail notice Sharapova received about the policy change did not get her attention, a circumstance most adults can sympathize with.

Doping controversies are not limited to Olympic athletes. The 2017 Reebok CrossFit Games disqualified men's third place finisher Ricky Garard and two other competitors. In 2005, the U.S. Congress held hearings about steroid misuse in Major League Baseball. Star witness Jose Canseco had written a provocative book asserting many MLB players had used steroids to improve their results. The hearing also included testimony from parents of two young athletes who had committed suicide after suffering side effects from steroids.

The extraordinary complexity and expense of investigating and countering artificial performance enhancements has ripple effects that make managing the Olympics and other sports organizations even more complicated. The field of sports analytics shows great promise in discovering game plans most likely to succeed. But data that has been corrupted by secretive doping practices is a poor foundation. If corrupted data produces further errors on a regular basis, those failures unsettle potential investors in the sports analytics field. That, in turn, makes it more difficult for other sports ventures to raise capital or sell their companies.

Honest individual athletes seeking sponsorship support or new jobs can also face difficulties if doping by other athletes taints the image of their sport or a national team. Even Olympic legend Usain Bolt lost a medal as a result of cheating by another athlete. The IOC's sample retesting program determined that in 2008 Bolt's 100-meter relay teammate, Nesta Carter, had used the banned stimulant methylhexaneamine. Bolt won gold in the same event in 2012 and 2016, but he also had to win six other gold medals to secure his distinction as the most successful runner in modern Olympic history.

Hitting the Wall

Endurance athletes can relate to fatigue wearing down parts of the Olympic community as controversies continue. Many call the feeling "hitting the wall" as fatigue sets in when some limits to endurance are reached.

In 2017, John Weston Parry published a critical look at athlete health and welfare called "The Athlete's Dilemma" which highlighted the serious consequences of sacrificing athlete's health for competitive advantages in sports. Understanding these challenges will be necessary to benefit from sports technology's advances in health and human performance, as well as to maintain the credibility of Olympic values.

Many observations by Parry and independent researchers sharing his perspectives should encourage the Olympic sports community to adapt to limits on human performance and aim for higher standards of athlete health:

- Repeated sports related concussions have been found to impair brain functions and in more severe cases to cause brain damage or neurological disorders.
- Performance enhancing drugs and recreational drugs can aggravate the seriousness of sports injuries.
- Most sports federations do not have comprehensive strategies for helping athletes who were severely injured in sports competitions after their sports careers.
- Peak volumes of testing for prohibited substances at the Olympics can lead to delays up to four days for results to be reported.
- Components of some over-the-counter cold and allergy medications can result in findings of prohibited substances in cases where athletes were not systematically doping or not even aware of banned substance exposure.
- Confidential surveys of track and field athletes participating in World Championship events indicated that nearly 30 percent had tried some prohibited performance enhancing drugs at some point in their careers.

Practical challenges have made the official IOC antidoping policy of "zero tolerance" an elusive goal. In many cases, antidoping enforcement by National Olympic Committees has not worked effectively. Some cannot recruit enough adequately trained professionals. In addition, many elite athletes train at global centers of competence or with a coach based in a foreign country—or play for professional teams far away from their home country. Lengthy distances and infrequent personal contacts can make it more difficult for National Olympic Committee staff to complete all the tasks necessary for flawless antidoping compliance.

In addition to the complex issues surrounding performance enhancing drugs, the Olympic sports community has experienced "hitting the wall" style fatigue with a panoply of health issues, such as:

- "Relative Energy Deficiency in Sports," identified as a malady by an IOC working group, which found sports regimens causing diminished endurance, strength, and conditioning can result in depletion of nutritional energy reserves following sustained exertion.
- Runner's dystonia, which can cause high-performance runners to lose key abilities to coordinate mind functions with legs and feet and seriously degrade performance.
- Iliac artery endofibrosis, a repetitive stress injury aggravated by the leaning forward posture essential for high-performance cyclists, causing arterial disease and numbness for dozens of Olympic and professional cyclists.
- "The Female Athlete Triad," a set of unhealthy conditions for many female athletes whose bodies confront rigorous training and weight control regimens; typically these are eating disorders, irregular menstrual cycles, and depletion of bone strength.

The IOC, for its part, has made continued research regarding sports injuries, prevention, and treatment a priority. Starting in 2009, the IOC Medical and Scientific Commission has sought proposals for funding research from research institutes, teaching hospitals, and universities and awarded four-year grants up to U.S. $100,000 for selected research projects.

New Challenges

Some of the most inspiring stories from the Olympics feature Olympic athletes who try a completely different sport and do well enough to make the team. Lolo Jones of the United States competed in athletics at the 2008 and 2012 Summer Olympics. Jones also won gold medals at the

2008 and 2010 World Indoor Championships. In 2013, she took on the new challenge of competing in bobsleigh and won a gold medal at the 2013 mixed team event of the International Bobsleigh World Championships, which qualified her for Sochi 2014.

Pita Taufatofua hails from the small island nation of Tonga in the South Pacific and had never seen snow. Taufatofua became a standout at the 2018 Winter Olympics. After qualifying to compete in taekwondo at the Rio 2016 Summer Olympics, he sought the new—and unprecedented—challenge of qualifying to compete in Nordic skiing. Taufatofua just barely managed to qualify for the Winter Olympics and did not win a medal, but he inspired many others to believe that almost any challenge can be mastered.

Lolo Jones, Pita Taufatofua, and other Olympians with similar confidence will not lack for challenges if their next goal is to help the Olympics move past some of the chaos at several other sports organizations. The IOC and host city organizers have no direct control over other sports organizations, so this is no easy task. The individual cases involve enough issues for individual books of their own. Reviewing a few of the most notorious cases shows how problems arise and challenge the Olympic sports community's image and credibility.

FIFA, the international football sports federation, organizes many top tier international competitions, as well as youth development programs. The FIFA Men's World Cup is the most viewed international sports event after the Summer Olympics itself. But another kind of international team—lawyers, auditors, and law enforcement agents—found that key managers and board directors at FIFA had surpassed the limits of inept financial management to reach criminal misconduct.

In 2015, the U.S. Department of Justice charged 14 FIFA leaders serving as either senior executives or board directors with racketeering, wire fraud, and money laundering. Twenty-seven other defendants were also charged. The indictment listed a total of 47 criminal violations over 24 years. The estimated total of bribes and kickbacks paid by organizations to enter into contracts with FIFA exceeded $150 million. In addition, longtime FIFA President Sepp Blatter and former FIFA consultant Michel Platini were disciplined and banned from football for eight years following investigation of an unusual payment of $2 million from FIFA to Platini. Several defendants entered guilty pleas that acknowledged widespread financial mismanagement and disregard for traditional Olympic values.

Several top tier FIFA sponsors discontinued their support—Sony, Johnson & Johnson, and Emirates Airlines, followed by McDonald's after the 2018 Men's World Cup. Other sponsors, including VISA and Coca-Cola, publicly criticized FIFA. Prominent sports business leaders began talking openly about "negative equity" and the risks that negative news about FIFA could damage support for other sports.

But considering the scale of charges against many FIFA leaders and the seriousness of many of their confessions, the organization and the sports world demonstrated impressive resilience. The 2015 FIFA Women's World Cup in Canada set new records for viewing of football matches in the United States and Japan. FIFA broadened its sponsorship base with Qatar Airlines and Wanda Group of China, owner of the worldwide IRONMAN series and Chinese professional sports teams.

The 2018 FIFA Men's World Cup set records for financial success and strengthened FIFA's financial foundation. Total revenues exceeded $6 billion, up 25 percent from the 2014 FIFA Men's World Cup in Brazil. Estimated broadcast revenues reached $3 billion, based on a global audience of 3.2 million spectators. FIFA maintained over $4 billion in financial reserves and resources to invest over $1 billion annually in sports development programs, primarily in low-income countries with limited sports infrastructures. The FIFA brand continued to resonate with consumers. The FIFA 18 official-licensed video game sold over 24 million copies during its release and the FIFA mobile app was installed on 193 million smartphones, setting categorywide records.

The Olympic community approached the FIFA crisis cautiously, reaffirming the long-standing tradition of sports organization autonomy, but signaling displeasure with the admonition "enough is enough." FIFA's embattled President Joseph Blatter had served as a voting member of the IOC from 1999 to 2015 but declined to run for another term. His successor, Gianni Infantino, was not nominated to serve on the IOC, a subtle signal that the Olympic community sought to distance itself from FIFA for a suitable period while continuing to manage all key activities needed to include football at future Summer Olympic Games.

While many leaders in the Olympic community might wish that the widespread criminal misconduct that surfaced at FIFA had been a single, isolated incident, further investigations uncovered more challenges.

The sports under the aegis of the International Association of Athletic Federations (IAAF) are widely considered the foundation of Olympic sports. Discus throws, long jumps, and foot races trace their origins to the ancient Olympics and the first modern Olympics. The series of scandals at the IAAF, followed by criminal prosecutions, sent shockwaves through the Olympic community.

Following multiple allegations of financial misconduct, former long jumper Lamine Diack resigned under pressure as IAAF president in 2015. He had been IAAF president for 16 years, as well as a voting member of the International Olympic Committee from 1999 to 2014. Diack openly admitted to earning over $14 million in consulting fees in addition to his salary during his tenure as IAAF president.

The consulting fee controversies at IAAF have been a recurring theme in the sports world. Sports agents and promoters have valuable contacts and rare deal making skills. Many have seen compensation grow as marketing rights became more valuable. There is no universal standard for a consulting fee so high that it constitutes an outright bribe. The range of market rate commissions the general public sees is wide. An agent representing a seller in a real estate transaction would typically receive 2 to 3 percent of the transaction value. Commissions in art sales are typically over 10 percent. Advertising agencies typically charge 15 percent for media purchases. Legal forms of "dual agency" in which one party represents both buyer and seller exist in most countries.

Diack did receive a reprimand and a warning from the IOC Executive Committee in 2011 after a bankruptcy proceeding revealed substantial payments to him by an IAAF business partner. But he continued to serve his term as a voting member of the IOC. And he made a good effort to donate substantial sums to charities and youth organizations, so that his public image was acceptable to many.

After Diack completed his IOC member term in 2014 and became an honorary member, the scale of corruption charges increased and was followed by multiple criminal allegations. A $2 million payment to a company controlled by Diack for creation of a new athletics event series in Africa appeared to financial investigators as excessive to the point of criminal misconduct, particularly since the event series did not move off the drawing board.

In addition, several athletes who failed doping tests reported that Diack had pulled strings to conceal cheating, permitting the athletes to continue competing in exchange for payments to bank accounts controlled by Diack or his close business associates. The evidence convinced French prosecutors to arrest him in November 2015, after which the IOC Executive Committee voted to end his honorary member status. Then, in June 2018, French prosecutors charged Diack with breach of trust at the expense of the IAAF.

The IAAF, much like FIFA, demonstrated resolve and resilience. The 2017 IAAF World Championships were noted in the *Guinness Book of World Records* for the most tickets sold for a single venue sporting event—705,000. Online views of clips from the World Championships reached the 1.6 billion mark. Top tier global brands Asics, Seiko, TDK, and Australia's QNB Bank supported the IAAF with sponsorship packages valued at over $100 million each.

In 2018, tennis shattered IAAF's 2017 attendance record when 732,663 spectators viewed the Fiftieth Anniversary of the U.S. Open of Tennis in Forest Hills. The enthusiasm of these fans and many others brushed off a series of match fixing scandals involving so many players that it might qualify for a different entry in the *Guinness Book of Records*.

In January 2019, Europol, the European Union law enforcement agency, announced 83 arrests related to its investigation of an international syndicate bribing tennis players to intentionally lose matches in order to generate big winnings through rigged sports betting. This followed 13 arrests in Belgium on similar charges. In addition, the Tennis Integrity Unit of the International Tennis Union had already published case materials detailing dozens of suspensions or bans of players involved in match fixing confirmed by the Court for Arbitration of Sports.

It is common knowledge that similar challenges have been reported in other Olympic sports. The Olympics' ability to maintain its popularity and engage additional support from a growing list of prestigious sponsors has demonstrated more than public relations expertise. Many financial analysts use the term "bulletproof" when an enterprise emerges from a series of crises unscathed or even stronger.

There are other institutions which have not demonstrated the resilience of Olympic sports when confronted with comparable crises. The public accounting firm Arthur Andersen, once among the world's top five, was forced to liquidate in 2002 following several cases of careless auditing and reporting, including headline making bankruptcies at Enron and Worldcom. This eliminated many units of the company which had not been involved in dubious business practices.

The exceptional ability of Olympic sports to jump very high hurdles is based on much more than a strong brand and many unique, sustainable competitive advantages. A strong ecosystem on the business side and a strong community on the personal side have proven their value time and again. But vocal objections to bid city proposals have become a sign that even the Olympics must adapt to changing times. That story is evolving, too, and one more factor that keeps Olympic sports a center of attention worldwide.

A Case in Point: The Toronto 2015 Pan American Games

Discouraging reports of spiraling costs and budget excesses at past Olympic Games have been a major factor in dissuading potential host communities from moving forward with Olympic plans. Many successful international multisport competitions have not received as much attention. The Toronto 2015 edition of the Pan American Games, the third largest international sports event, took place close to original budget estimates and "without a hitch" in the words of the official audit report. The presidents of the Pan American Sports Organization (PASO) and International Paralympic Committee expressed complete satisfaction with the results.

Toronto 2015 demonstrated pragmatic approaches matching new directions emphasized by Paris 2024 and Los Angeles 2028 organizers. Many could become standard practices in the future.

The smooth functioning of all key events and functions at Toronto 2015 demonstrated many elements of standardization of international multisport events modeled after the Olympics. This standardization made it less complicated to plan and complete many essential support activities, including:

- Producing opening and closing ceremonies
- Customizing facilities for 51 sports and reconditioning after the Games
- Designing and producing medals
- Establishing a temporary international press center
- Subcontracting ticket sales
- Executing a branding, licensing, and merchandizing program
- Arranging multiple corporate sponsorship programs
- Carrying out an idyllic, inclusive torch relay and related cultural festival
- Drug testing with minimal controversy, 20 disqualifications (0.26 percent), and no arbitration cases
- Security which prevented any major incidents at official Toronto 2015 events
- Comprehensive quality control to ensure that 28 sports met qualification criteria for Rio 2016
- Hosting organizational meetings for PASO and International Sports Federations

The sponsorship program included classic lead generation opportunities brought up to date with mobile phone apps. These built valuable databases of qualified prospects' e-mail and mobile phone contacts. In addition, the marketing team reached out to a high-potential segment for sports sponsorships, companies which seek to recruit athletes as employees. As Japan, the United States, and other economies consider solutions for projected labor shortages, other host committees can follow this lead.

Plans for the Athlete's Village changed modestly. The original plan envisioned a high-performance athlete training center with outdoor fields on site. No design fit the available property, but existing university and commercial facilities met all practical requirements. The conversion of the Athlete's Village to private ownership went smoothly and 92 percent of the units sold quickly, avoiding any need for temporary subsidies.

The Toronto 2015 volunteer program took sports event management to the next level and became a model quickly adopted by the 2016 and 2020 Summer Olympics organizing committees. Toronto 2015 took advantage of innovative communications technology from sponsor Cisco to open volunteer recruiting globally. This brought in thousands of volunteers with relevant experience at prior Olympics, Pan American Games, and Commonwealth Games who shared their experience with newer volunteers and helped to train the local talent pool, one of the key legacy goals of the entire hosting program.

The final total operating costs of Toronto 2015 came in just above U.S. $1.8 billion. That figure reflected expenditures per athlete around U.S. $235,000, a figure similar to London 2012 and Rio 2016, as well as the plan for Tokyo 2020.

Postgames conversion of athletic facilities for use by students and the general public upgraded the region's infrastructure both for sports and for the broader field of health and human performance. The main PanAm sports facility became the sports center of the University of Toronto Scarborough campus as well as a high-performance sports training center for the province of Ontario. York University also converted facilities to use as a high-performance athletics center and converted a new stadium to private use. Collectively, these facilities can educate professionals to train tens of thousands of local residents with fitness programs.

The Toronto 2015 program demonstrated how public–private partnerships can work. Municipal and provincial governments funded the costs of infrastructure that would remain a public asset after the games. A private developer assumed responsibility for converting and selling the facilities that local governments did not retain. In addition, private sector sponsors covered most of the operating costs, supplemented by event ticket sales and merchandising. All revenues for broadcast rights went directly to PASO, which follows the IOC model to redistribute available revenues for sports training programs.

Beyond modern infrastructure projects that will continue to benefit the region, Toronto strengthened its brand in the sports business community to help attract new business. Successfully hosting the world's third largest international multisport event demonstrated that Toronto can provide both the scale and the expertise needed to accommodate almost any sports project.

Illustration 4.1 Good collaboration skills have helped many IOC members to craft solutions for serious challenges and demonstrate impressive resilience.

Key Sources and References

AT Kearny. August 2014. "Winning in the Business of Sports." Online Publication: https://atkearney.com/communications-media-technology/article?/a/winning-in-the-business-of-sports

Beacher, R. September 2018. "Tomorrow Belongs to those Who are Active Today." *Olympic Review*, no. 108, pp. 70–73.

Cappello, J.C. Summer 2013. "Despite FIFA's Problems, Billions Around the World Continue to be Enthralled by the Beautiful Game." *America's Quarterly*.

De Souza, M.J., A. Nattiv, E. Joy, M. Misra, N. Williams, R.J. Mallinson, and E. Panel. 2013. "2014 Female Athlete Triad Coalition Consensus Statement on Treatment and Return to Play of the Female Athlete Triad." *British Journal of Sports Medicine* 48, no. 4, pp. 289–289.

Fidelity Investments. "Healthcare Technology." Online Publication (Updated Daily): https://eresearch.fidelity.com/eresearch/markets_sectors/sectors/sectors_in_market.jhtml?tab=industries&sector=35

Flyvbjerg, B., A. Stewart, and A. Budzier. July 1, 2016. "The Oxford Olympics Study 2016: Cost and Cost Overrun at the Games." University of Oxford, Saïd Business School. Research Papers online Publication: https://papers.ssrn.com/sol3/papers.cfm?abstract_id=2804554

Gibson, O. 2012. "Doping at the Olympics: Are We Winning the War on Drugs?" *The Guardian*, July 31.

Hilmes, O. February 2018. *Berlin 1936: Sixteen Days in August.* London: Penguin Random House.

Insurify Insights. June 4, 2018. "The 10 States with the Most Suspended/Revoked Licenses." Online Publication: https://insurify.com/insights/the-10-states-with-the-most-suspended-revoked-licenses/

International Olympic Committee. July 19, 2019. Press Release: "Beijing 2022 Shows Positive Impact of Games Vision." https://olympic.org/news/beijing-2022-shows-positive-impact-of-games-vision

Jean Carlet. President - World Alliance Against Antimicrobial Resistance. March 1, 2018. "AMR Control 2018." Online Publication: http://resistancecontrol.info/wpcontent/uploads/2019/03/AMR2018_march1.pdf

Lang, A. November 16, 2018. "Calgary Residents Kibosh Potential Olympic Bid." *Bloomberg Markets.* Online Publication: https://bnnbloomberg.ca/video/calgary-residents-kibosh-potential-olympic-bid-1542048

Leicester, J. June 24, 2019. "France to Try Former IAAF Boss Diack and his Son." *AP News.* Online Publication: https://apnews.com/062b33a2819f4149bb8f3ea1ab16ad61

McGroarty, B. October 16, 2018. "Wellness Now a $4.2 Trillion Global Industry – with 12.8% Growth from 2015 to 2017." Online Publication: https://globalwellnessinstitute.org/press-room/press-releases/wellness-now-a-4-2-trillion-global-industry

MSN Sport (Australia). June 2, 2015. "FIFA Crisis and Sports Scandals through History." Online Publication: https://msn.com/en-au/sport/more-sports/fifa-crisis-and-sports-scandals-through-history/ss-BBkBj2U#image=1

Office of the Auditor General of Ontario. June 2016. "2015 Pan Am/ Parapan Am Games." Online Publication: http://auditor.on.ca/en/content/specialreports/specialreports/2015panam_june2016_en.pdf

Parry, J.W. June 2017. *The Athlete's Dilemma.* Rowman & Littlefield Publishers.

Peter Wallace – Toronto City Manager. June 2016. "Staff report on Pan Am / Parapan Am Games Capital Program & Community Initiatives." Online Publication: https://toronto.ca/legdocs/mmis/2016/ex/bgrd/backgroundfile-90747.pdf

Sheinin, D. 2005. "Baseball Has a Day of Reckoning In Congress: McGwire Remains Evasive During Steroid Testimony." *Washington Post*, March 18.

Smith, R. 2018. "Was Russia 2018 the Greatest of All World Cups?" *The New York Times*, July 13.

Spiegel Staff Co-authors. August 17, 2009. "The Price of Gold: The Legacy of Doping in the GDR." *Der Spiegel*, Hamburg, Germany.

Sylt, C. March 18, 2018. "AEG Books $200 Million In Profits On London's O2 Arena." *Forbes Online.* Online Publication: https://forbes.com/sites/csylt/2018/03/18/aeg-books-200-million-profits-on-londons-o2-arena/#a1cb6994af36

Team GB. May 30, 2013. "London 2012 Publishes its Final Report And Accounts." Online Publication: https://teamgb.com/news/london-2012-publishes-its-final-report-and-accounts

Tsukuba International Academy for Sport Studies (TIAS). 2017. "Tsukuba International Academy for Sport Studies (TIAS) Hosts 'Tri-university Showcase Conference,' on SFT Sport Academy Formation Project." *PR Newswire*, December 21.

U.S. Bureau of Labor Statistics. May 2018. "National Industry-Specific Occupational Employment and Wage Estimates." NAICS 711200 – Spectator Sports. Online Publication: https://bls.gov/oes/current/naics4_711200.htm#31-0000

Yamaguchi, M. 2017. "The Cost of the Tokyo 2020 Olympics has Already Nearly Doubled to $12.6 Billion." *Associated Press*, June 6.

CHAPTER 5

From Rio to Tokyo—
Charting a New Course

Trial and Error

In 2009, U.S. President Barack Obama was inaugurated in January and honored with the Nobel Peace Prize in December. The Nobel Committee distinguished President Obama for his "extraordinary efforts to strengthen international diplomacy and cooperation between peoples." His efforts included a polished presentation to the International Olympic Committee about the strengths of Chicago to host the 2016 Summer Olympic Games. The president and First Lady Michelle Obama also met personally with many IOC members and highlighted Mrs. Obama's dedication to promoting youth sports programs.

Two-thirds of IOC members who voted to select the winning bid chose Rio de Janeiro. The press events that followed and interviews with individual members of the IOC focused on the positive aspects of Rio's bid and enthusiasm for hosting the Olympic Games in South America for the first time. Brazil's President Lula da Silva joined Rio 2016 Committee leader Carlos Nuzman, Rio de Janeiro State Governor Sergio Cabral, and Rio Mayor Eduardo Paes for iconic photos celebrating the victory.

Ten years later, da Silva, Nuzman, and Cabral were disgraced with bribery and corruption charges and some hefty penalties. Former President da Silva's conviction involved acceptance of real estate from a government contractor seeking favors and was unrelated to the Olympics. Former President da Silva was released from prison in November 2019 following a decision by Brazil's Supreme Court. Cabral was sentenced to a total of 59 years in prison for leading a criminal organization, accepting kickbacks, and money laundering.

Eduardo Paes ran for election to replace Cabral and lost by a 20 percent margin. His campaign had claimed that the Rio 2016 Olympics had covered its costs and left infrastructure improvements which benefitted 3 million residents. *Sports Illustrated* reported different results with photos and descriptions of a dozen Rio 2016 facilities later shut down and vacant or in disrepair.

The most serious charges against Nuzman were passive corruption, criminal organization, and money laundering. The key evidence was $2 million deposited in a foreign bank account Nuzman controlled. Nuzman, already in his 70s, was confined under house arrest, replaced as president of the Brazilian Olympic Committee, and suspended as an honorary member of the IOC.

This was not good news for either the International Olympic Committee or the Olympic sports community. The prevailing response was to "keep calm and carry on." Problems that had surfaced before they passed the threshold of serious criminal convictions had already started a cycle of change. Management journals describe this as "business process re-engineering." In the Olympic world, the efforts were branded *Agenda 2020*. Initially approved by the full IOC membership in 2014, the title recognized that it would take five or six years to achieve key goals.

The path forward spotlighted the resilience that is a hallmark of the best parts of the Olympic community. It also concretely demonstrated the value that many athletes and managers attribute to learning from mistakes. Two-time Olympic gold medalist Abby Wambach devoted an entire chapter of her 2019 bestseller "Wolfpack" to this subject called "Make Failure Your Fuel." In 2018, *Men's Health* magazine featured Instagram fitness guru Carlos Marti Garcia with his motto "Mistakes make me fitter," and chronicled the ways this CrossFit expert has improved his fitness routines through trial and error. Sports marketing authority Jean-Claude Biver distinguished the ability of athletes to learn from mistakes on their paths to excellence in his 2018 marketing guide.

The Most Perfect Imperfect Olympics

IOC President Thomas Bach described the 2016 Rio Olympics as "the most perfect imperfect Olympics." It was a diplomatic way to describe an ambitious plan that went far off course as the local economy tumbled and the host nation experienced unprecedented political chaos. Much like a team that trails behind throughout a match and then miraculously scores a winning goal in the final seconds, Rio 2016 delivered a vibrant Olympics that captivated a large global television audience of 3.5 billion. Once again, the Olympics had an opportunity to demonstrate its resilience and it did just that.

While negative news reports impacted public views of the Rio 2016 Olympics, the event actually set records for setting records—27 world records and 91 Olympic records in the Summer Olympics alone. The Rio 2016 Paralympics took this to the next level with 220 new world records and 432 new Paralympic records. Attendance set records, too, at 2.15 million. Rio 2016 also set a record for an Olympic merchandising campaign. Licensing revenues reached the $321 million mark, double the previous record achieved at Beijing 2008.

Broadcasting of the Rio 2016 Olympics set scores of records, including a 97 percent increase from 2012 in the number of hours of programming transmitted by official broadcasters and a total of 357,000 hours of total coverage. These set both Olympic and world records. This pattern repeated itself in countries around the world. In Brazil, the Olympics television viewing audience reached a record of 86 million, a 117 percent increase. In Canada, the Olympic television viewing audience grew to a record 32.1 million.

Rio 2016 also reported a 200 percent increase over London 2012 in hours of digital programming for Internet channels. The 243,000-hour figure set another record. There were 4 billion individual views of the IOC's own official website, Olympic.org, twice the volume reported at London 2012. Social media channels shared a total of 7 billion video clips from official Olympics sources—media partners, Olympic Broadcasting Services, sponsors, Olympic teams, and the IOC's own YouTube channel. This foundation boosted the launch of the Olympic Channel, which began broadcasting the day after the Rio 2016 closing ceremony. In the following two years, the channel acquired 3 million subscribers.

The plan for Rio 2016 positioned 37 athletic facilities throughout a large metropolitan area eight times the size of New York City. This took advantage of some existing facilities, such as Maracana stadium, which was remodeled to serve as the Olympic Stadium. The plan also envisioned Olympic facilities as a foundation to make sports more accessible to different communities throughout the metropolitan area.

The Rio 2016 plan also necessitated significant additions to the area's transport infrastructure. There were many good reasons to upgrade regional transport links. But scheduling these projects before the Olympics at the same time the international airport expanded and hotel construction boomed strained many resources.

Sometimes the strain was too much. A recreational bike path designed to connect the sports cluster in the Copacabana Beach area with the Barra district's Olympic arenas collapsed in April 2016, just three months after opening. Two cyclists died and there was no way to repair the damage before the Olympic cycling road race planned for the adjacent elevated road. The bike path had been built with the aim of strengthening the sports facility legacy of Rio 2016.

The tragic deaths of the cyclists were not the only fatalities in the news. In March 2016, Rio de Janeiro released a report citing 11 deaths of construction workers engaged in 2016 Olympics projects. The report pointed out that there had been zero construction-related fatalities at London 2012.

The nosedive experienced by the national economy of Brazil and the local economy of Rio de Janeiro was not part of the original Rio 2016 proposal submitted seven years earlier, but it was a harsh reality that made adaptability essential. From the end of 2014 to the end of 2016, the national economy declined by 8 percent. Unemployment rose to 12.6 percent. The Moody's and Standard and Poor's debt rating agencies cut Brazil's credit rating from just barely investment grade to "junk" status.

The Rio de Janeiro area was particularly hard hit, because most of its economic activity depended on oil production, petrochemicals, and raw materials exports, three businesses that saw severe declines when commodity prices dropped in late 2014.

The economic crisis was accompanied by political turmoil. Brazil's President Dilma Rousseff, who had been a dependable supporter of plans for Rio 2016, was impeached. The mechanics of the impeachment process meant that Vice President Michel Temer was initially appointed to serve as president for 180 days while the impeachment process took place, including the Rio 2016 Olympics. Temer fulfilled the ceremonial duties of head of state under these awkward circumstances and ultimately became president until 2018.

Rio 2016's well-publicized difficulties tested the popular adage that "there is no such thing as bad publicity." The *New York Times* told its readers "As the Olympics Near, Brazil and Rio Let the Bad Times Roll." Canada's *National Post* marked the Hundred Days to Go countdown with the discouraging headline "When it comes to dire Olympic predictions, Rio 2016 checks all the boxes 100 days before Games." A week before the Games officially began, the UK-based *Guardian* covered a gruesome example with a story titled "Second fire at Olympic Village adds to woes of Rio 2016 organisers."

The Olympic spirit prevailed. From an energetic opening ceremony that featured icons of Brazil's heritage to a closing ceremony that welcomed Tokyo as a successor, television audiences saw the Olympics excel. Almost every detail went according to plan, and when that did not happen, there was some other good news to celebrate. Seven Olympic teams won their first gold medals and 7 billion video clips from Olympic broadcasters circulated on social media. Nothing succeeds like success.

Testing a New Course With Agenda 2020 and the New Norm

Steady improvement is valued in the Olympic community, if not always achieved. The record expenditures at Sochi 2014, as well as the financial and management difficulties that surfaced at Rio 2016, reflected trends that had been developing over years. These prompted discussions in the media, government agencies, the sports industry, and general public. The IOC responded with a set of policies it called *Agenda 2020*, approved by its voting members in December 2014. As the title suggests, the program was designed with a vision of the future and an expectation that it would take several years to implement.

Recent Olympics in Sochi and Beijing had reported exceptionally high total outlays for preparations to host the Olympic Games. Significant sums were invested in infrastructure projects such as airport renovations and transit links planned for use long after the Games themselves had ended—but many potential host cities and countries could not finance any project on that scale, regardless of how large future benefits might be. That financial reality conflicted with the Olympic goals of inclusiveness and promoting sports worldwide.

The *Agenda 2020* program aspired to enable more cities to host the Olympic Games. This strategy outlined a process for separating the operating costs of hosting the Olympics which would be funded in part by the IOC from infrastructure projects to be financed by local governments and private companies. But this could not change the financial challenge that multibillion dollar projects require large upfront expenditures even when future benefits continue for many years.

Practical details limit the latitude of the IOC and prospective host cities to optimize bidding and hosting activities that are essential for each presentation of the Olympic Games. The lead time required by the IOC's tradition of awarding the games 7 years in advance is 10 years or longer. It often takes a year for the National Olympic Committee to select a bid city and then two years to compete with other candidates. The total time is longer than many government officials hold their positions.

In addition, there is no practical alternative to a host city after selection, because lead times are so long no other city could take on all the responsibilities. That is different than smaller events which are sometimes compelled to find an alternative. Guadalajara won the bid to host FINA's 2017 World Aquatics Championships but could not secure financing. Afterwards, FINA sought a replacement capable of maintaining the biennial event schedule and Budapest managed the program as initially planned.

Currently, lead times for some Olympic bids are increasing. In January 2019, the U.S. Olympic Committee selected Salt Lake City as a candidate to prepare a bid to host the 2030 Winter Olympics. In February 2019, the Korean Sport and Olympic Committee authorized Seoul to draw up plans for hosting the 2032 Summer Olympics.

Agenda 2020 promoted a special focus on sustainability and legacy. Ideally, this would maximize use of existing facilities while new facilities focus on legacy projects with high potential for productive use many years after the Games. Some success stories demonstrate that Olympic Games venues can be used far into the future. Olympic stadiums and training facilities from the Rome 1960 Summer Olympics and Tokyo 1964 Olympics are still in use today. The Tokyo 1964 Olympic Park also serves as a heliport and logistics center for emergency response teams.

But images of former Olympic sports facilities fallen into disrepair detract from the Olympic brand and pose an ongoing public relations challenge to local host city bid advocates. In August 2016, Mashable contributor Tim Chester published an illustrated feature of 17 former Olympic venues that aged badly and were no longer usable and contrasted photos of decay with relics from the ancient Olympic Games. In 2018, National Geographic published an illustrated guide to abandoned Olympic stadiums. Similar reports are common when local media outlets cover potential Olympic host city proposals from their local areas.

Agenda 2020 inspired changes aimed to make qualified host city proposals less expensive, but even optimistic forecasts of future host city expenditures involve billions of dollars—and require capacity to finance the expenditures. Los Angeles presented a bid which emphasized using existing facilities and arranging for private organizations to take over new construction projects. Nonetheless, initial bid cost estimates topped $5 billion, not including security costs to be funded by the federal government. Subsequently, the official LA 2028 budget announced in April 2019 increased to $6.9 billion, following an independent evaluation by financial analysts at KPMG.

In 2019, Los Angeles had a Moody's bond rating of Aa2—the third highest grade— and could issue general obligation bonds if necessary. But Hungary, which ultimately withdrew a proposal for Budapest to host the 2024 Summer Games, had a credit rating that was barely investment grade because public debt levels were already high. Senegal, selected to host the 2023 Summer Youth Olympic Games, has had a credit rating of Ba3. That is two levels below the lowest level of investment grade debt, so Senegal could not depend on access to bond markets if Olympics related spending exceeded government resources.

The IOC cannot influence host city access to debt markets. But it can modify the Olympics' scale, which has a strong impact on total expenditures required. *Agenda 2020* opted for almost no growth in the number of sports, events, or athletes competing and advocated reducing other accredited personnel slots. The plan also allowed local organizers to propose up to five additional sports for a guest appearance. These additions would require IOC approval and private sponsorships that would not impact the host city budget.

While cost control is a routine—and sometimes essential—approach to financial management, spending to increase total market size has been the foundation of many success stories. The classic example in management texts is Henry Ford's decision to double the daily wage Ford paid factory workers, so that they could afford to buy a Ford car, building momentum for future market growth. *Agenda 2020* initiatives of promoting gender equality and eliminating any barriers to participation related to sexual orientation have similar upside potential. For sponsors in directly related sports businesses, such as running shoes or tennis racquets, the benefits are easy to calculate. Double the market size and then add modest increases in expenses for product development and marketing, so that profit margins and revenues improve significantly.

In practice, increasing participation in sports requires years of planning and training. Key steps include identifying talented athletes, arranging quality coaching and professional education, meeting standards for Olympic qualifying events, and fundraising. This foundation was already in place by the time of Rio 2016, when participation by female athletes crossed the 45 percent threshold.

Agenda 2020 advanced other initiatives for promoting participation in sports and was able to demonstrate impressive results. It advocated expansion of Olympic education programs and the launch of a new Olympic Channel for year-round coverage of Olympic sports and athletes. Seven million Brazilian students participated in Olympic education programs funded by private sponsors the year before Rio 2016. By the start of 2019, 17,240 schools throughout Japan, both public and private, had received official status to teach formal Olympic education programs. The Olympic Channel signed up 3 million subscribers to its own digital platform in its first two years of operation and added content distribution with many broadcasters, including Eurosport, beIN Sports, and Amazon Fire TV.

Agenda 2020's initiatives for controlling or eliminating the disruption from performance enhancing drugs and cheating schemes have been overshadowed by negative reports that show the scale of the problem is very large compared to the resources devoted to controlling doping. While the terms used in the IOC's official policy had good intentions, the calls to "protect clean athletes" and "honor clean athletes" have been difficult to transform into action.

One aspect of the policy to honor clean athletes who were designated medal winners after the initial medal winners were disqualified for doping became impossible to implement. The series "The Complete Guide to the Olympics" was discontinued in 2016. Veteran author and Olympic historian David Wallechinsky remarked sadly, "let's face it, had I published a book this year, the 98 plus new doping positives would have rendered it already out-of-date."

The Agenda 2020 plan had to handle a delicate balancing act between securing the support of existing IOC members and increasing opportunities to recruit new members with different expertise relevant to important sports trends. The plan set a retirement age of 70, with a provision that five exceptions could be made at each full meeting of IOC members. This increased the ability to recruit new members with specialized professional expertise that could assist the IOC's efforts to implement its new agenda.

Implementation of Agenda 2020 retirement age limits and recruiting replacements proved difficult. Four years after the December 2014 IOC Session which approved policy changes, the IOC had 20 vacancies to fill to reach its stated membership goal of 115. One objective of establishing a retirement age of 70—with provisions for a few exceptions if needed—was to increase the capacity to recruit new voting members with specialized expertise relevant to key changes expected in the future. The IOC also seeks broad geographical representation in its membership. While the Olympic community attracts people who thrive on new challenges, this particular challenge has been too tough for many Olympic athletes and esteemed world leaders currently serving on the IOC.

Agenda 2020 earned serious attention in the sporting world, but the general public barely noticed. The polished video introducing its goals posted on YouTube in November 2014 received 13,000 views and 14 likes during the following four years. By contrast, the complete video of the London 2012 Opening Ceremony achieved 10 million views and the segment featuring Queen Elizabeth II with movie idol Daniel Craig surpassed 22 million views in the following six years.

The decline in interest in hosting the Olympic Games was unmistakable. After Rome, Hamburg, and Budapest withdrew bids to host the 2024 Summer Olympics, only Paris and Los Angeles were able to finalize their proposals and secure the necessary support. The IOC scheduled a special session in July 2017 to approve both proposals at the same time, selecting Paris for 2024 and Los Angeles for 2028.

Following the awards to Paris and Los Angeles, Olympic leaders refocused on pragmatic solutions to make hosting the Olympics more appealing to residents of potential host cities. The program was given the title *The New Norm* and highlighted flexibility and feasibility. Advocates forecast that the set of 118 policies could reduce Summer Olympic Games costs by as much as $1 billion and cut future Winter Olympic Games by one-half billion dollars.

The New Norm was approved by the full IOC membership at its 2018 session preceding the 2018 Winter Olympics in Pyeongchang. It went beyond policy goals to introduce specific, actionable measures to substantially reduce the costs of future Olympics. The steps outlined mirrored trends in the business world to reduce duplication of tasks and increase operating efficiency. These included consolidating games information services, ticketing, and customer database management in IOC-managed business units, separating these costs from local organizing committee budgets. The New Norm also underscored the priority of sustainability policies at the IOC and outlined specific measures to increase energy efficiency.

The New Norm vision of savings for test events was modest and focused on improving operational efficiency. This solidified the importance of test event programs in improving production quality and staff preparedness at the actual Olympic Games and reinforced the trend of the Olympics featuring year-round activities and educational programs.

While the 2018 Winter Olympics attracted global attention, the *New Norm* business policies remained a subject for sports industry specialists. A professionally designed video introduction posted by IOC Media on YouTube registered about 1,500 views and 20 likes. During this period, the Olympic Channel's post of Pyeongchang 2018 highlights received over 600,000 views. Although Los Angeles had already been selected to host the 2028 Olympics in July 2017 and stood to benefit from cost savings of up to $1 billion, the *Los Angeles Daily News* did not publish a single report about *The New Norm*.

The sports insiders who did follow the significant changes put forth in the *New Norm* program had great expectations. The Beijing 2022 Organizing Committee established a legacy commission in November 2018 directed to incorporate the *New Norm* policies in its long-term planning. Swedish Olympic Committee President Mats Årjes promoted the benefits in media events organized to win greater public support for the Stockholm 2026 Winter Olympics proposal.

Two details in the IOC's published financial statements indicate that the Olympics does have valuable resources to systematically and permanently reduce the costs of producing the Olympics with policies like those outlined in *The New Norm*:

- First, the productivity of the IOC's own employees is exceptionally high, surpassing 98 percent of the multinationals in the Standard and Poor's 500. Talent and leadership play an important role in this achievement, but the IOC also benefits substantially from transfer of expertise from TOP sponsors at no cost to the IOC. Since the number of TOP sponsors has increased steadily and the commitments continue into the next decade, this competitive advantage is positioned to continue.

- Second, the IOC has no outside debt at all. While the IOC does report modest short-term payment obligations to affiliated organizations, it has no bank debt. This is not unusual at nonprofit foundations, but corporations which manage commercial activities such as those planned in The New Norm often use the related assets as security for lenders and free up funds for other programs. Live Nation, which owns and operates Ticketmaster, has $2 of long-term debt for every dollar in equity on its balance sheet. The company's scale is comparable to the Olympics in total and its total long-term debt at the end of 2018 was $2.7 billion.

The controversial challenges related to prohibited performance enhancing drugs and medical treatments were not targeted for cost reductions. New policies designed to improve efficiency and accelerate handling of individual cases were put in place during and after the 2018 Winter Olympics. This effort promoted a new global organization, chartered as a nonprofit foundation, called the Independent Testing Agency (ITA).

The ITA's objective is to consolidate all the expertise needed to discourage contamination of international sporting competitions with prohibited performance enhancements and protect innocent athletes who carefully comply with the rules. Sports event organizers and international sports federations will still need to play an essential role in communicating the rules to the athletes, while the ITA implements tests and reports findings. Implementation of the interface between sports federations and the ITA remains a moving target.

Ideally, the ITA will be free of the pressures which international sports federations and national counterparts face when promoting participation and a good image for sports. The Olympics and Olympic qualifying events are a cornerstone of its future, effectively serving as reference clients.

More than 200 National Olympic Committees and 63 designated Olympic sports collectively make the need for coordination by ITA staff a complex task. Sophisticated technologies and database management methods have the potential to help manage that complexity, but achievement of the official "zero tolerance" policy will require at least as much effort as winning an Olympic gold medal. According to statistics published by WADA in 2016, the rate of "adverse analytical findings" was 1 percent for tests of athletes competing in Olympic sports, comparable to the rate reported in 2012. WADA and other experts are quick to point out that these kinds of test results do not automatically indicate intentional violation of doping rules or grounds for sanctions. But they keep the case load for further investigation at burdensome levels.

Disturbing doping cases continued to be reported and showed that business as usual could not be an effective solution. U.S. swimmer and 12-time Olympic medal winner Ryan Lochte was suspended in 2018 after he posted a photo of himself during a prohibited blood doping treatment. Austrian cross-country skier Johannes Dürr, who was disqualified at Sochi 2014 for failing an EPO blood doping test and later sanctioned by the IOC Disciplinary Commission, shared an inside look at athlete doping for a documentary by German broadcaster ARD in 2018. The details led the Austrian Federal Police to investigate a clinic and five athletes who continued banned blood doping, followed by nine arrests. In March 2019, the IOC sanctioned an additional three athletes from

London 2012 following retesting of samples that provided more evidence of banned doping, bringing total London 2012 sanctions to date to 116.

Given the reality that hundreds of Olympic athletes have been sanctioned for misuse of performance enhancing drugs and treatments in the last decade, bolstering the mechanisms for investigating suspects and sanctioning those found guilty has emerged as a top priority. The consensus solution was to centralize authority at a permanent division of the Court for Arbitration of Sports and try a fast track style approach.

Under the new case management system implemented in 2019, athletes charged with a doping violation have the choice of having their case heard quickly by a single arbitrator, whose ruling could be appealed to a panel of three arbitrators. Or the athlete can choose to appear before a panel of three arbitrators and waive any right to an appeal. Athletes are not required to be represented by an attorney, but those who can afford one or obtain legal insurance will be a step ahead.

Testing Limits at Pyeongchang 2018

On January 20, 2018, just three weeks before the start of the 2018 Winter Olympic Games, Olympic representatives from both North and South Korea met with Olympic leaders and Pyeongchang 2018 executives at IOC headquarters in Lausanne, Switzerland. In a few hours they crafted an historic agreement enabling dozens of athletes, journalists, coaches, and other supporters from North Korea to participate in the 2018 Winter Olympic Games. A few exceptions were made—and made graciously—to make this nearly impossible last-minute addition to the Games a reality, but the Olympic spirit prevailed in a way that left everyone celebrating success.

This impressive achievement demonstrated many of the strengths the Olympic community relies upon to deal with tough challenges. Leaders were able to reach agreements quickly and put them into action quickly. Just 12 days later, the main delegation from North Korea arrived in Pyeongchang, South Korea, to join fellow North Korean athletes who were already training on-site as part of a unified Women's Ice Hockey team with athletes from both North and South Korea. The fast pace matched Olympic traditions and the motto "Faster, Higher, Stronger."

These exceptional developments helped to demonstrate the value of the Olympic Games and spotlight their values. The inspirational values of the Olympic community had already made many impossible moments possible for more than a century. The "Olympic Truce," which aims to inspire nations to set aside their differences in the spirit of the Olympic Games, had surpassed another limit.

The local team which organized the Pyeongchang 2018 Winter Olympics also surpassed its marketing targets, securing commitments for $1.8 billion in sponsorships. This helped the organization report a surplus from the operations of the Games and generate funds to promote sports training in the future. The official accounting reported after the Games ended was total revenues of $2.245 billion and total expenditures of $2.190 billion, creating a surplus of $55 million. The IOC executive board voted to use the surplus to create a foundation to support sports development programs in Korea.

The official accounting also yielded $430 million from the IOC's own broadcast and marketing revenues to be distributed to the international federations organizing Olympic Winter sports and National Olympic Committees. For smaller NOCs, this makes an important difference. The National Olympic Committee of Lithuania, for example, has an annual budget of approximately $7 million. Lithuania devotes much of the funding to training and travel by athletes, but also funds grant programs for sports training outreach activities for the general public and youth sports programs.

Good news from Pyeongchang 2018 was welcome but did not present an immediate solution for reutilizing all of the larger facilities after the Games concluded. In March 2019, the IOC reported that the former International Broadcast Centre (IBC) would become a national archive for the National Library of Korea and the former Pyeongchang 2018 Organizing Committee headquarters would be converted to use as a winter sports training center. Accommodations at the Athlete's Village and Media Village were all sold as private residences. But the estimated cost of maintaining the sports venues was $18 million a year. No private contractor had made a commitment for these operations before the Games took place and even one year later, no private contractor had stepped forth.

A respectable number of potential host cities looked past the challenges Rio 2016 and Pyeongchang 2018 had faced and expressed serious interest in hosting the Olympic Games in the future. Indonesia's ambassador to Switzerland submitted a formal bid letter from President Joko Widodo to the International Olympic Committee in February 2019.

Less than respectable controversies at several affiliated sports organizations continued to divert attention from the ambitious future goals of Olympic leaders. International Biathlon Union President Anders Besseberg and Secretary General Nicole Resch resigned in 2019 after both were charged with fraud and corruption while overlooking doping violations by Russian athletes. The IBU had previously suspended the Russian Biathlon Union as details of the doping schemes emerged.

The problems reported at the sports federation handling Olympic Boxing, AIBA, were so serious that the IOC Executive Committee suspended AIBA's Olympic accreditation and suspended IOC revenue sharing payments. AIBA already had $16 million in debt on its books and was effectively insolvent. Auditors from EY declined to approve AIBA's published financial statements and reported "uncertainty still persists about the ability of the organisation to continue as a going concern." AIBA was not able to open a bank account in Switzerland, where its headquarters were based. The IOC ultimately disassociated the Olympics from AIBA and transferred responsibility for managing boxing competitions at the 2020 Olympics to a special task force.

These kinds of difficulties had the potential to erode the Olympics' audience and brand value, but that did not happen at all. On the contrary, the confidence and resilience factors which have distinguished the Olympics in the past rose to new heights. A March 2018 survey of 36,000 adults in 16 countries by Publicis Sport and Entertainment reported that 93 percent of respondents recognized the Olympic brand and symbols and the entire group ranked the Olympics second worldwide for general appeal. The report also confirmed that the global television audience for the 2018 Winter Olympics had reached 1.92 billion, a record for winter sports coverage.

Getting Set for Tokyo 2020

The Tokyo 2020 Olympics had a long head start. Tokyo's bid committee to compete for the 2016 Summer Olympics was launched in August 2006. The 2016 bid ranked behind Rio and Madrid in votes, but it provided lessons a new team used in preparing a new bid for 2020. A key concept of the 2016 bid carried forward to Tokyo 2020. That was to connect two clusters of facilities. The first would be a "Heritage Zone" centered around landmarks from the 1964 Tokyo Olympic Games and Japan's Imperial Palace. The second would feature new construction close to Tokyo Bay with a distinctive contemporary look.

While the heritage of the Tokyo 1964 Summer Olympics was a foundation of the plan for Tokyo 2020, the Olympic tradition of adaptiveness became a strong influence. First, key policy changes approved by the IOC at its 127th Session in 2014 promoting the *Agenda 2020* recommendations motivated a series of modifications to the original plan. Second, more and more of the expertise employed to produce the Olympics was based on the know-how and teamwork of experienced veterans who had worked on previous editions of the Olympic Games. Together, these trends encouraged tried and tested practices used to plan and manage the Olympic Games, promoting efficiency through standardization.

The Olympic tradition of knowledge sharing has helped to build a talent pool with distinctive competence and the Tokyo 2020 team is using this expertise as a foundation. Experienced Olympics veterans are working for Tokyo 2020 in many different functions, such as

- Tokyo 2020 Senior Director Competition Planning, previously Rio 2016 Sports Entries Manager, London 2012 Sports Entries Advisor, Innsbruck 2012 YOG Sports Entries Consultant, Singapore 2010 YOG Head of Entries and Results, Beijing 2008 Consultant, and Athens 2004 Entries Manager
- Tokyo 2020 Director National Paralympic Committee Relations, previously Pyeongchang 2018 Head of NOC/NPC Relations, Rio 2016 NOC/NPC Services Manager, Sochi 2014 Organizing Committee NOC/NPC Communications

Consultant, and London 2012 NOC/NPC Communications
Manager

- Tokyo 2020 Olympic Applications Project Manager and
  Consultant, previously Rio 2016 Games Management System
  Manager and London 2012 Games Management Systems
  Manager
- Tokyo 2020 Sport Entries Senior Manager, previously Rio
  2016 Sport Entries Continental Coordinator—Asia
- Tokyo 2020 Project Director of Sport Planning, previously
  Rio 2016 Sport Operations Centre Manager
- Tokyo 2020 Technology Project Management Office Project
  Director, previously Rio 2016 Technology Project Manage-
  ment Office Program Manager
- Tokyo 2020 Ticketing Client Group International Sales
  Director, previously Rio 2016 Ticketing Coordinator and
  2014 FIFA World Cup Accommodation Office Venue Liaison
  Manager

Many other Tokyo 2020 executives are regular full-time employees of
Tokyo 2020 sponsors such as the Dentsu advertising agency and NTT,
a large telecommunications and network management enterprise. They
work as "loaned" employees, reporting to the Tokyo 2020 management
team. Often, they have had extensive prior experience as loaned employees at other international sports events held in Japan. This approach to
human resources does not have a long history at the Olympics, but if it
produces good results at Tokyo 2020, it can become one more practice
that Olympics managers can put to work in the future.

Experience makes a difference. But in the case of Tokyo 2020, the
aspirations of *Agenda 2020* and *The New Norm* do not stand out. And
once again, controversy has surrounded some expenditure projections
substantially higher than original estimates. By January 2019, when
Tokyo 2020 leaders released an updated forecast, total operating expenses
including temporary customization of facilities reached the $12.4 bil-
lion mark. That was $5 billion more than the proposal submitted to
IOC members in 2013, when Tokyo was selected as 2020 host city. The

headline the *Washington Post* chose to report this development was not flattering: "To the surprise of no one, the 2020 Tokyo Olympics are going massively over budget."

Adjusting Tokyo 2020 expenditures for long-term improvements to the metropolitan area's assets and potential tax receipts will be difficult for the most talented financial analysts. Most of the new facilities being constructed in the Tokyo Bay Zone are adding two to three meters of surface in order to be at least six meters above sea level. This storm surge protection will make the area safer and more valuable for hundreds of years, not just during the Olympics. The technological expertise which sponsors accumulate in specialized activities such as weather forecasting tools, 8K high-definition broadcasting, and 5G wireless network operation generates corporate income tax revenues when the sponsors market this know-how to commercial clients. And the contact lists of ticket buyers, registrations for free events, and social media subscriptions have substantial commercial value; LiveNation, the parent company of Ticketmaster, surpassed a total market value of $13.5 billion in 2019, based largely on the value of its customer lists, social media contacts, and technological expertise.

Tokyo 2020 leaders have made efforts to address cost concerns by highlighting potential benefits. The idea of presenting Tokyo 2020 as a "Recovery Olympics" which can bring optimism to the earthquake- and tsunami-devastated region north of Tokyo has won both supporters and detractors. The March 2011 disaster resulted in more than 20,000 fatalities, 2,500 missing persons, and $300 billion in property damage. The Official Tokyo 2020 Olympic torch relay will begin in the area and a softball match scheduled for a newly built stadium in Fukushima will be the first official Tokyo 2020 competition. But Japan has had a shortage of skilled construction workers and some area residents feel reconstruction of the disaster hit area should take priority over new construction for Olympics facilities.

Tokyo 2020 is also being positioned as a showcase for environment friendly sustainability programs and innovative uses of intriguing technologies. The sustainability plan features a recycling program for electronic devices to source gold, silver, and bronze for Tokyo 2020 medals, repurposing of timber used at temporary venues, and renewable energy installations at all new venues.

A report published by the American Chamber of Commerce in Japan highlighted leading edge technologies that will attract attention at Tokyo 2020:

- Precision laser measurement systems for evaluation by sports event judges
- Software-defined traffic management systems
- Hydrogen fueled vehicles and autonomous vehicles
- Integrated 5G network communications
- Robots designed to assist hospitality services

A global audience for impressive technologies has also been a favorable selling point in recruiting Tokyo 2020 sponsors, since exporting sophisticated technology components and software is one of Japan's largest and most profitable industries.

Opportunities to showcase Japan's culture and style are adding momentum to a worldwide fascination with Japan. In the past decade, Japan advanced from being an exotic travel destination to one of the world's top 10. Many first-time visitors seek attractions inspired by anime characters, popular culture, and digital arts. New Olympic landmarks will add to the attraction.

Most Olympic fans will view Tokyo 2020 presented by large broadcast teams dedicated to using the Olympics to spotlight their talent. Plans for Tokyo 2020 include an array of high-definition, virtual reality, and panoramic screen technologies designed to impress and amaze. Media companies are also aiming to appeal to viewers across the entire range of digital media and give them the experience of being part of a community.

In 2020, the Olympic community and the Olympic viewing audience are set to be larger than ever. The combination of tried and tested practices together with innovative new technologies is scaling up to handle this challenge. Like the Olympics itself, this challenge will be a focus of global attention.

A Case in Point: World Baseball and Softball Confederation's Road to Tokyo

Managing complex relationships has become important for sports federation managers to achieve their goals and win support in the Olympic community. The case of the World Baseball Softball Confederation's efforts to be included at future Summer Olympic Games illustrates how sports federations can navigate complicated networks of relationships and achieve multiple goals.

While baseball and softball are among the most popular sports in the world and baseball is considered the national sport of 2020 Summer Olympics host country Japan, the International Olympic Committee dropped both baseball and softball from the Olympic sports roster following the Beijing 2008 Olympics. The "Agenda 2020" initiatives in December 2014 opened a new door for baseball and softball to be included at the Tokyo 2020 Olympics at the recommendation of the local organizing committee for this edition of the Olympic Games.

Public support for adding baseball and softball to the schedule of the Tokyo 2020 Olympics was more than enthusiastic. The proposal dominated local media coverage of plans for the Olympics. But only the IOC Congress had final authority to approve local host city proposals to invite new sports. Support from other IOC members and National Olympic Committees based in countries where baseball and softball are popular boosted the idea.

Without Olympic revenue sharing or grants from Olympic solidarity after 2008, funding was modest. Both the baseball and softball communities saw the potential benefits of pooling their resources. The two separate organizations launched a single World Baseball Softball Confederation in 2013, with the goal of completely integrating their activities and building a unique brand over the next five years.

Sports federations seeking selection as Olympic sports must have the ability to organize Olympic qualifying events. By organizing series of world championships, supported with sponsors and broadcast rights managed by WBSC, the confederation demonstrated its ability to achieve this goal and built helpful connections to win support for a return to the Olympic program. Much of this activity was also complementary to the main function of official international sports federations—building participation and audiences for their sports. The federations are rewarded with a valuable competitive advantage, an exclusive right to organize the rules, schedules, and communications for international competitions.

WBSC President Riccardo Fraccari credited two initiatives with building a good base of world championship events. First, connections with professional sports leagues were strengthened by inviting them to become associate members of the confederation. Then host city bidding competitions and broadcast contracts built a foundation for long-term financial stability and increased staff support to maintain key connections. Achieving agreements with many different parties who literally span the globe became a key success factor for WBSC—and also a core competence of the organization.

The steps followed to build support to gain a new Olympic invitation created new opportunities, but also required resources and connections. This made it essential to win contacts with key influencers and more visibility in social media and mainstream sports news.

By 2015, WBSC's initiatives provided enough resources to improve staffing and conduct board meetings twice a year for faster decision making. This helped efforts to include baseball and softball in the 2020 Summer Olympic program. The IOC itself typically meets once a year, while its Executive Board holds quarterly meetings. The period between the approval of the proposal to empower the local organizing committee to invite WBSC and other selected sports federations to Tokyo 2020 was just 20 months. WBSC had to plan and secure funding for the Olympic qualifying events in addition to convincing key decision makers to support the Tokyo 2020 proposal for additional sports. Faster decision making and additional resources, plus the experience of organizing world championships, helped this initiative succeed.

The new invitation for baseball and softball to take part in the Tokyo 2020 Olympics brought the additional advantages of motivating the national federations participating in the WBSC, but status as an additional sport for Tokyo 2020 did not provide any IOC revenue sharing benefits. WBSC leaders needed to craft a new game plan at the March 2018 meeting of the WBSC Board of Directors. This was held in Paris, recently selected as the host city for the 2024 Summer Olympics.

WBSC arranged to hold the March 2018 board meeting at the offices of the French Olympic Committee and invited Denis Masseglia, president of France Olympique, to open the meeting. The strategic choice of venue also provided an opportunity for meetings with decision makers in the Paris 2024 team and France's Minister of Sports, Laura Flessel. Flessel was a politician from the French overseas region of Guadeloupe, a Caribbean island where baseball and softball are popular. This approach demonstrated how WBSC has found ways to advocate for its sport while it had limited resources and influence over Olympic decision making.

An invitation from Paris 2024 would need extra effort. The Paris 2024 concept is to use existing or temporary facilities, so securing a venue will require advance planning and sponsor support. At the same time, WBSC has an opportunity to position an invitation to baseball and softball for the Paris 2024 Olympics as a foundation for continuity between 2020 host city Tokyo and 2028 host city Los Angeles, two global centers of excellence in these sports.

The Paris meeting also presented a key strategic initiative designed to consolidate the advantages WBSC had gained since 2013 and strengthen its brand and image. The longer-term vision for WBSC includes the goal of positioning baseball and softball as a lifestyle brand with its large community of followers. WSBC attracted tens of thousands of followers on Twitter and over 400,0000 on Facebook. WBSC's image and prestige benefitted from the honor of softball's selection to be the first event at Tokyo 2020.

The Paris Executive Board meeting also marked an historic step for the sport of Baseball Softball with the establishment of Baseball5 as an official discipline of the WBSC. Baseball5 came to life after nearly two years of research and pilot projects with the aim of developing a new discipline that would massively increase the accessibility to the sport. Baseball5 or B5 is a 5-on-5 street version of Baseball Softball which is more affordable and can be played virtually everywhere requiring only a flat surface and a rubber ball. Presented as a mixed discipline with urban flavor and focused on enhancing the youth appeal of Baseball Softball, the Baseball5 initiative is yet another example of how the WBSC governing body moves to align its strategy with that of the broader Olympic Movement and its goals for increased accessibility to sport, gender balance, youth appeal and sustainability.

Illustration 5.1 Paris Mayor Anne Hidalgo (left) and the Paris 2024 team are applying the experience of earlier Olympics host cities.

In 2018, WBSC founded BASE a media-marketing company in charge of monetizing the media and sponsorship rights of the federation. This platform will increase visibility for WBSC events and secure future financing with subscription revenues. It will also present an opportunity to reinforce the professional appearance of WBSC events and help cost savings in the production of individual events by sharing a common infrastructure and shared staff expertise.

Converting the popularity of individual athletes into audience growth and leveraging larger audiences to increase sponsorship support can add competitive advantages. But WBSC's leaders will need to continue to rely on their ability to build support in the larger sports community to be considered for inclusion in future Summer Olympics programs.

Key Sources and References

Associated Press. April 21, 2016. "At Least Two Dead as Bike Lane Built Ahead of Rio Games Collapses." Online Publication: https://nationalpost.com/sports/olympics/at-least-two-dead-as-bike-lane-built-ahead-of-rio-games-collapses

Balch, O. 2016. "What Happens to Olympic Venues After the Closing Ceremony?" *The Guardian*, September 1.

BBC News. March 7, 2017. "Brazil's Recession Worst on Record." Online Publication: https://bbc.com/news/business-39193748

Butler, N. February 6, 2019. "IOC Launch Reforms They Claim Could Save Cities Hosting the Olympics $1 Billion." Online Publication: https://insidethegames.biz/articles/1061122/ioc-launch-reforms-they-claim-could-save-cities-hosting-the-olympics-1-billion

Chester, T. August 10, 2016. "Abandoned Olympic Venues." Online Publication: https://mashable.com/2016/08/10/abandoned-olympic-venues/?europe=true#puDVJYnddqq7

Cheyney, M. March 2018. "Games of Growth: How the Olympics Help Develop Cities." *The ACCJ Journal.*

CNN Library. March 4, 2019. "2011 Japan Earthquake - Tsunami Fast Facts." Online Publication: https://edition.cnn.com/2013/07/17/world/asia/japan-earthquake---tsunami-fast-facts/index.html

ESPN.com news services. April 26, 2016. "Rio Auditor Says 11 Workers Killed During Olympic Construction." Online Publication: https://espn.com/olympics/story/_/id/15357163/11-workers-killed-olympic-construction-brazil

International Olympic Committee. 2017. "Global Broadcast and Audience Report Rio 2016."

International Olympic Committee. 2017. "Marketing Report Rio 2016."

International Olympic Committee. December 2014. "Olympic Agenda 2020: 20 + 20 Recommendations."

International Olympic Committee. July 2019. "IOC Annual Report 2018 Credibility, Sustainability, Youth."

Mackay, D. February 9, 2019. "Behind Positive Headlines for Role in Korean Peace Process, There Lies Uncomfortable Truth for IOC about Pyeongchang 2018." Online Publication: https://insidethegames.biz/articles/1075318/duncan-mackay-behind-positive-headlines-for-role-in-korean-peace-process-there-lies-uncomfortable-truth-for-ioc-about-pyeongchang-2018

Osaki, T. 2019. "Coming Events Give Japan Chance to Shine as Travel Destination." *Japan Times,* February 19.

Panja, T. 2019. "From Boston, Witness in Rio Olympics Bribery Case has his Day in Court." *The New York Times,* May 17.

Pavitt, M. August 28, 2018. "Former Rio Mayor Defends 2016 Olympic Legacy and Denies Debts Remain." Online Publication: https://insidethegames.biz/articles/1069320/former-rio-mayor-defends-2016-olympic-legacy-and-denies-debts-remain

Somvichian-Clausen, A. February 2018. "Look Inside the Abandoned Stadiums of Past Olympics." *National Geographic.* Online Publication: https://nationalgeographic.com/photography/proof/2018/february/old-abandoned-olympic-stadiums/

Washington Post Sports. October 9, 2018. "To the Surprise of No One the Tokyo 2020 Olympics are Going Massively Over Budget." *Washington*

Post. Online Publication: https://washingtonpost.com/sports/2018/10/09/surprise-no-one-tokyo-olympics-are-going-massively-overbudget/?utm_term=.24d028855309

World Baseball Softball Confederation. March 23, 2018. "WBSC Executive Board Meeting Live On YouTube." Archived Video: http://wbsc.org/wbsc-executive-board-meeting-live-on-youtube/

CHAPTER 6

The Media Is the Message

Building Value and Building Momentum

The 2032 Summer Olympic Games are far in the future. But in May 2014, broadcast chiefs at NBC Universal were so confident the event would generate top-quality material that they agreed to pay $7.75 billion for Olympic broadcast rights in the United States from 2022 to 2032. That figure was substantially more than the $50,000 rival network CBS paid for U.S. broadcast rights at the 1960 Winter Olympics in Squaw Valley or the $1.2 million total revenues the Olympics received for broadcast rights to cover the 1960 Summer Olympics in Rome, when just 21 nations broadcast the Games on television.

The value of Olympic broadcast rights has increased steadily and steeply. Total revenues were $17.8 million for Munich in 1972, $286.9 million for Los Angeles in 1984, $818.3 million for Atlanta in 1996, and $1.74 billion for Beijing in 2008. Increases continued through the Rio 2016 Summer Olympics, which generated $2.87 billion in broadcast rights fees.

Why is Olympic media so valuable today? The "nothing succeeds like success" track record of the Olympics has built positive momentum. And the standardized, tried, and tested practices used to plan and manage media production at the Olympics have become so dependable that media executives are confident they will work well two decades later. Polished attention to detail and pageantry at Olympic events has become a notable advantage in the media world.

Veteran Sports Illustrated Photography Director Steve Fine credits the vibrant imagery of the Olympics as the strength which sets it apart from other sports events. The value the Olympics adds to the media world is substantial. Expertise built at the Olympic Games is a foundation for quality production of other sports programs at over 60 networks designated as official Olympic rights holding broadcasters and at over 500 channels which broadcast Olympics programming.

Rapid change in the media industry has made the learning agility promoted by the Olympics even more valuable. In 1999, the population of U.S. consumers with a television in their home was 98 percent. That figure declined to 88 percent over the next 20 years as the popularity of computers, tablets, and other digital devices for viewing programming— including the Olympics—increased. In 2012, the number of U.S. viewers registered to view the Olympics on smartphones reached 10 million.

Mass audiences viewing the Olympics on digital devices have become a worldwide trend. This substantially increased total viewing of the Olympics and archived programs after the Games conclude. Online views of clips and news at the IOC's own website, Olympic.org., doubled from London 2012 to reach 26 million during the Rio 2016 Summer Games. Seven Networks, the official Olympics broadcaster in Australia, live-streamed more than 100 million minutes of coverage. Seventy-six million subscribers in Europe viewed Olympic coverage on the Eurosport digital player.

Setting the Pace

If there were no Olympic Games, the television and radio industries would still exist today. But they would not be the same. That is because, time and again, the critical mass of having so many technical and production experts together in one place at one time working on one project raises innovation and production standards to higher levels. For example:

- The development of the first instant replay system began at the 1960 Winter Olympics in Squaw Valley.
- The first International Broadcast Center for a sports event was built for the 1964 Winter Olympics in Innsbruck, a model subsequently adopted by the FIFA World Cup.
- International live broadcasts via satellite began at the 1964 Tokyo Summer Olympics.

- High-definition television (HDTV) had its commercial debut at the 1984 Los Angeles Summer Games.
- Network engineers at the 1984 Los Angeles Summer Games pioneered the deployment of large-scale multipoint fiber optic networks for live video transmission to television editors.
- Global high-definition digital video production started at the Barcelona 1992 Summer Olympics.
- The DVCPRO 50 format was first tested at the Olympic Winter Games Nagano 1998, reducing recording times by 50 percent.
- At the Sydney 2000 Games in 2000, Orad Hi-Tec Systems conducted the first successful trial of real-time superimposition of graphical images on video frames, letting viewers see finish lines, world record lines, and other key comparisons not visible to stadium viewers.
- The 2006 Winter Olympic Games in Torino featured a synchronized audio amplification system designed exclusively for the Olympic Games by TOP sponsor Panasonic.
- Underwater robotic cameras with zoom in, tilt, spin, and angle calibration features debuted at the London 2012 Summer Olympic Games.
- A Sochi 2014 display was the first use of the brand new PT-DZ21KE, a projector with a brightness of 20,000 lumens.
- During the 2018 Winter Olympic Games, CBC, Canadian Broadcasting Corporation, introduced the first live streaming of select Olympic competitions via Twitter, integrated with a viewership promotion strategy.
- Pyeongchang 2018 also presented the first trial of live 4K high-definition 360-degree view cameras.

Tokyo 2020 test events have also provided a valuable test for application of cloud technology. This enables efficient and customized use of Olympic video feeds by international broadcasters. Production staff at individual television studios operated by hundreds of channels showing coverage of the Olympic Games will be able to access and edit video feeds from Tokyo in their own offices and own time zones, greatly increasing productivity and reducing business travel costs.

Technological innovation at the Olympics has been accompanied by unmatched scale. The production of video from the 2008 Beijing Summer Olympics employed 1,000 cameras, 350 remote broadcast units, and 64 mobile broadcast vans.

In addition to innovations which television viewers do see, the Olympics drives innovative deployment of key broadcast support services which viewers do not see. Mobile and remote broadcast units need extensive temporary electrical power connections. In addition, transmission of thousands of hours of HDTV requires more intensive use of telecommunications networks than any other activity. Developing technical solutions to these challenges enhances expertise for managing other peak period demands, such as responding to an earthquake or tsunami as quickly as possible. This underscores the value of the Olympics' knowledge sharing capabilities.

Teamwork

The first world broadcaster briefing for the 2022 Winter Olympics in Beijing took place in February 2019, three years before the event itself. This level of advance preparation and teamwork has become standard for media organizations which present the Olympics. The largest are "Rights Holding Broadcasters" (RHBs). Many invest hundreds of millions of dollars for broadcast rights alone and then dedicate staff to plan in advance for high-quality programming.

Quality production uses a talent pool that epitomizes the phrase "a cast of thousands." The official Broadcast Training Program run by Olympic Broadcast Services has prepared over 11,000 specialists to date and is gearing up for another 2,000 at Tokyo 2020. Viewers see on-camera reporters and interviewers, as well as an occasional videographer. Behind the scenes, many specialists work together to manage every detail to deliver uniformly high quality:

- **Editorial and commentary teams:** program producers, program presenters, interviewers, sports expert commentators, announcers, sports and athlete research writers, interview question writers, wardrobe coordinators, stylists, music library coordinators, social media content producers, documentary producers

- **Production teams:** Dolby sound engineers, audio-video synchronization technicians, music montage mixers, broadcast engineers, radio frequency engineers, lighting technicians, still photographers, videographers, video editors, video overlay designers, commentary system audio operators, animation engineers, graphic designers, set designers, set managers, transmission controllers, robotic camera maintenance personnel, drone camera technicians, repair technicians, results reporting system managers

- **Business support teams:** systems engineers, acoustical engineers, quality assurance testers, information technology hardware integration engineers, software installation and maintenance professionals, Internet service installation technicians, cybersecurity agents, password administrators, air-conditioning and ventilation technicians, vehicle fleet managers, temporary office space designers, construction managers, data analysts, scheduling managers

- **Sports and ceremony venue managers:** program managers, temporary telecommunications and electrical network installation personnel, press room managers, press conference and mixed zone facility managers, volunteer coordinators, hospitality staff, maintenance and repair professionals, cleaning staff, prop installers

- **Administration:** accreditation managers, food and beverage managers, payroll managers, payments processors, bookkeepers, budget managers, purchasing managers, inventory managers, leasing managers, contract administrators, transportation vendor managers, shipping clerks, copyright and trademark compliance managers, document production and printing staff, translators, protocol officers, liaison officers

TOP Olympic partners contribute more to these team efforts. Over 30 years from 1988 to 2018, Panasonic loaned and maintained 1,581 recorders, 841 video cameras, and 7,400 monitors. Panasonic technicians also install high-capacity audio systems at dozens of venues during each Olympic Games. Omega experts have managed the timing and results reporting systems used by broadcasters.

The Olympics' history and the achievements of Olympic athletes have built a strong brand. But the image that is projected by exceptional team-work and attention to detail behind the presentation of the Olympics to audiences around the world adds even more value. And the practice that the media teams accumulate during two years of test events leading up to the Olympics improves results.

While competition and changing industry dynamics have caused sig-nificant cost pressures in sports journalism, this pressure has favored the Olympics in many cases. Olympic sports have instant recognition and dedicated followings. National Olympic Committees as well as Interna-tional Sports Federations have press departments which produce a steady stream of quality material. This makes it much easier to plan media cal-endars and promote highly publicized countdown campaigns such as the Olympic torch relay. And the 21st Century convention of channeling news with hashtags makes promoting Olympic coverage even easier.

Social media news feeds have also become an effective audience building tool. In 2019, NBC Olympics had 3.5 million followers on Facebook and over 900,000 on its Tokyo 2020 Twitter newsfeed, while in Canada, CBC Olympics surpassed 150,000 followers on Facebook. CONI, Italy's main Olympic organization, surpassed 200,000 followers in 2019. By early 2019, the IOC's own social media footprint reached 18 million followers on Facebook and 6 million on Twitter.

The team behind the team in Olympics broadcasting and media is almost unseen. In select countries, such as the United States and Japan, IOC executives enter into agreements with broadcast industry titans which operate multiple channels and manage every detail of Olympics coverage in their exclusive territories. But in the past decade, more and more agreements were reached with regional networks such as Eurosport, which covers 48 countries in Europe. Eurosport guarantees substantial fixed payments to the IOC and then selectively sublicenses some Olym-pic broadcast rights to sports channels with local strengths, such as France Television. This approach has expanded the Olympics' talent pool.

The combination of regional and local broadcasters and the growth of cable systems with higher channel capacities made it possible for the total number of channels covering the Olympics to double in the last decade. While 240 television channels around the world broadcasted the Vancouver 2010 Winter Olympics, Sochi 2014 broadcasts were featured on a total of 464 channels. Over 500 channels showed Rio 2016 broadcasts.

The long-term economic value of the Olympics to RHBs goes far beyond the profits they can earn by selling advertising and sponsorships during the games themselves. The Olympics is a powerful audience building tool and provides a range of opportunities to increase the attention viewers pay to official broadcasters. The 2018 Winter Olympics results showed:

- In Canada, Olympics broadcasts of official broadcaster CBC reached 85 percent of the population.
- In the United States, NBC Olympics signed up tens of millions of new users for its NBC Sports app.
- Across Europe, Eurosport reported a 166 percent volume increase for its digital device app in just one month.
- In Norway, TV Norge set a record for audience share at 93 percent when it broadcast the Olympic men's final 4 × 10 kilometer cross-country skiing relay.
- In Italy, official Olympics broadcaster RAI's average audience increased 500 percent.
- In Australia, official Olympic broadcaster Seven Network achieved a first place audience share ranking in every geographic market and every key demographic group.

Print media also provides extensive Olympics coverage, but the Internet has changed industry dynamics in print journalism dramatically. The *Philadelphia Inquirer* and *Philadelphia Daily News* filed for bankruptcy in February 2009. Tribune Media, owner of the *Chicago Tribune* and *Los Angeles Times*, underwent a bankruptcy reorganization in 2012. Over 100 American daily newspapers have stopped publishing entirely.

Search engines have become the primary means of finding sports news in this new environment and social media shares have become the primary means of gaining additional visibility. Leading international news agencies such as AP, UPI, AFP, and Reuters have distinct advantages reporting in this global news environment. With larger staffs than regional, single-language publications, they can cover more news in more languages in more countries.

Entrepreneurial news specialists have been agile enough to find audience focused niches in this changed environment. Bloggers publish online news and features for global audiences, focus on one or a few sport topics with dedicated followings, and surpass the news agencies with depth of coverage, insider reports, athlete profiles, advice columns, and reader participation. In one decade, many success stories have built audiences and strengthened Olympic goals for promoting sport worldwide. They cover a wide range of topics and enhance the knowledge sharing capabilities of Olympic sports:

- *GirlsWhoPoerlift.com* established a large following in the sports discipline of women's weightlifting and built a loyal readership with interactive features and special offers for members.
- *GamesBids.com* focused on a core audience of about 5,000 sports industry insiders dedicated to comprehensive coverage of bids for the Olympic Games and select international multisport events.
- *Handball Planet,* launched in 2010, attracted over 100,000 followers with independent reporting, interviews, and fan features.
- *InsideSport* built an online subscriber base of 1.5 million by providing comprehensive coverage of sports business in its home market of India and expanding internationally.
- *VeloNews,* a magazine, executed a classic product line extension strategy in digital media, reaching 2.3 million podcast downloads and 3.4 million video views in 2018.
- *Volleywood.net* built an online following of 800,000 positioned as a volleyball fan focused entertainment site.

Inside the Games, launched as an online publication in 2005, became the leading trade publication for Olympic sports business as an authoritative source for independent news. Access to key decision makers and exclusive interviews provided credibility and depth of coverage that regional news organizations could not match. Opinion pieces, guest columns, polls, and other interactive features added to the audience building approach. Comprehensive coverage combined with a site search feature made this online publication a convenient authoritative source.

As *Inside the Games'* ascent to leadership among sports event industry trade publications demonstrated, success in online sports publishing has taken effort, talent, meticulous organization, and good contacts. Not every story is a success story. Three similar international water polo blogs have been treading water competing for the same audience and the same sponsors. *Yahoo! Sports* built an impressive infrastructure for independent sports bloggers but it never reached a critical mass of readers or sponsors and the outside blogger program shut down in 2014.

Ice Network, which covered international ice skating, Olympic test events, and the Winter Olympics with Olympic accredited journalists, ceased operations in 2018. It had had to compete for audience attention with social media uploads and RHB webcasts and ultimately could not cover the costs of comprehensive reporting.

CyclingTV, founded in 2003, was originally hailed as a trendsetter, but never achieved critical mass to attract sponsors and finance quality content. Fifteen years later the channel had less than 11,000 followers on Facebook and Twitter combined. *CyclingTV's* inability to compete with online media content from *VeloNews* highlighted the critical importance of sports industry contacts and editorial expertise.

The Olympics has also supported a steady stream of books that interest large audiences. This maintains high awareness of the Olympics year round and not just during the Games. The Olympic World Library has 30,000 print publications and 8,900 e-documents in its collection. In 2019, Amazon.com listed over 2,000 titles currently for sale. Popular formats are "how to" tutorials, human interest, biography, success stories, self-help, inspiration, management, motivation, recipe books, art, and culture. The wide range of publications written about or authored by Olympic legends has had an impact similar to "surround sound" in the broadcast industry. This has built an unrivaled worldwide presence which professional sports leagues in single sports cannot match.

Featured book titles for World Book Day 2019 showed how Olympic-themed books can engage devoted audiences:

- *One Hundred Metres of Solitude*, the story of Usain Bolt
- *The Divine Comanici,* a portrait of the "perfect ten" gymnast
- *The Return of the King Kohei,* an audience builder for Tokyo 2020
- *Lolo Jones' Twitter Diary*, a new format to take readers behind the scenes of Olympic sports

Social media strengths extend the audience for Olympics themed books. Usain Bolt had 23 million followers by World Book Day in 2019. Nadia Comaneci had 300,000 followers four decades after her gold medal honors at the Montreal 1976 and Moscow 1980 Olympics.

All the components of Olympics media—books, news, video, podcasts, social media, and traditional television—have achieved success individually in their own categories. Collectively, they have reinforced the foundation of Olympics business success—unique, sustainable competitive advantages.

The Olympic Channel Adds New Dimensions

Launching an entirely new channel is not easy. Launching on a global scale to reach 200 countries with programming in a dozen languages is even more difficult. The launch of the Olympic Channel in 2016 faced another major challenge. Payments for regionally exclusive broadcast rights of the Olympic Games account for three-quarters of the IOC's revenues and support a significant share of the operating costs of the local organizing committees which present the Olympic Games. Preserving the primary source of income must be a high priority for any organization with ambitious future goals. The Olympic Channel has had to deliver visible benefits to RHBs while quickly achieving the scale to stay competitive in the sports broadcasting industry.

Results from the first two years showed this strategy was working and on course to develop opportunities at Tokyo 2020. Over 3 million subscribers signed up to watch free advertiser supported programming at the website portal, www.olympicchannel.com. In addition, many television channels and media subscription services have added Olympic Channel selections.

NBC Universal has a dedicated channel, also branded the Olympic Channel, available to over 35 million households through cable subscriptions. Claro Media Group, the official Olympic broadcaster in 17 Latin American countries, added the Olympic Channel, as did Grupo Globo, which covers Brazil. BeIN Sports has introduced the programs in 18 countries of the Middle East and North Africa region. A broadcaster consortium covers Japan.

Alibaba, one of the three founding sponsors of the Olympic Channel, joined with China's official Olympics broadcaster CCTV to launch a new Chinese television channel based on Olympic Channel programming. It customizes content to feature engaging stories about Chinese athletes and sports news. The new CCTV Olympic Channel in China was announced in January 2019.

By April 2019, agreements to feature programs from the Olympic Channel on traditional television covered over 160 countries. The Olympic Channel and Sony Pictures Network India began collaboration on year-round Olympic Channel highlights leading up to the 2020 Winter Youth Olympics and Summer Olympic Games. SportsMax signed up to make the Olympic Channel available in 22 Caribbean area countries it serves.

Agreements with digital media services are poised to give even more viewers access to Olympic Channel programs. New applications for Android TV and Apple TV debuted in 2019. In April 2019, the Roku online streaming service added the Olympic Channel for 24/7 viewing, plus access to archives of over 50 shows.

The Olympic Channel has built a foundation for content which complements official Olympics broadcasters by reinforcing the Olympic tradition of knowledge sharing. Social media sharing has made its format particularly well suited to knowledge sharing. This also matches "how to" style presentations and sports science topics.

Promoting Olympic sports and providing more visibility to sports events organized by international sports is an important mission of the

Olympics and stands alone as a valuable benefit. But giving sponsors a medium to reinforce the messages they promote together with Olympic content and build their brands with select audiences creates additional value. The three founding sponsors of the Olympic Channel—Toyota, Bridgestone, and Alibaba Group—have the marketing experience to optimize these benefits. But individual athletes, many just Olympic hopefuls patching together sports stipends, part-time earnings, and their own individual sponsorships, can also attract better sponsorship support with greater visibility from a dedicated Olympic Channel.

Sports broadcasting professionals who work on Olympic programming can leverage additional coverage in their preparation, presentation, and social media efforts. BeIN Sports, for example, engages 45 sports expert analysts, 54 commentators, and a dozen television program hosts for its traditional presentation of each Olympics. These professionals often need to prepare 10 hours for each hour they are actually on the air. And they must compete with broadcast giants like NBC and the BBC to get interviews with star athletes and material for feature programs. Broadening the assignment pool with year-round coverage based on The Olympic Channel rewards their investment in professional expertise and contacts focused on the Olympics.

Over two dozen production companies work on programming for the Olympic Channel. This is a cost-effective approach for covering news, events, and personalities that span the globe. It also builds international expertise regarding Olympic sports—a fundamental goal of the Olympics.

Social Media at the Next Level

Athletes have been popular social media subjects since the leading social media sites attracted mass audiences a decade ago. While charismatic cats and eyewitness reports of natural disasters can still win attention, professional production agencies and media consultants have focused on relevant opportunities to stand out in the crowded social media universe. YouTube alone averages over 1 billion video views per day. Athletes with compelling stories and authentic achievements have given social media professionalism and relevance, qualifying them to become social media influencers.

Social media consultant Sylvie Marchal coaches athletes to build on the confidence factors that promote their athletic success and to approach social media as a regimen with the same discipline as an athletic regimen. This typically means identifying a target audience, uploading a steady stream of relevant content, and interacting with followers—sharing greetings, thanks, helpful advice, and responses to messages.

Olympic athletes have advantages from association with a renowned brand and many choices to share professionally produced content from websites in the Olympic community. They are also conditioned to having every detail of their performance measured and reported. This can be a tough challenge for many others who seek social media success. But more than 15,000 athletes compete in each Olympiad, including Youth Olympic Games talent. And there are many more former Olympic athletes, coaches, and commentators, as well as Olympic hopefuls, so social media success has become a contest of its own.

Olympic learning agility gives a competitive edge on social media. That includes learning from other sites which appeal to their target audiences. They can also see what kinds of postings appeal to followers and the general public. The quantitative metrics of views, likes, comments, and replies can help. Moreover, the social skills athletes develop in sports are a natural match for social media. And athletes' achievements bring an authenticity that more commercial content rarely matches.

Sophisticated sponsors and media partners can leverage the competitive advantages which Olympic athletes bring to social media. In addition, staff at Olympic federations can often leverage athlete followings to strengthen their efforts to promote sports and physical fitness. A focused presence in social media supports good targeting of relevant geographic regions and demographic groups more dependably than mass media. Subtle inclusion of logos, images, and team colors reinforced by sincere communications gains authenticity in contrast to 30-second television spots or radio tunes. Instagram and YouTube have programs for sponsor product placement in content, accelerating this trend and providing prominent social media influencers with additional income.

Managing a high volume of contributors and activities in a media program is a complex task and requires a high degree of co-ordination. Not surprisingly, the range of success in building audiences on social media varies widely for sports organizations in the Olympic movement, as well as for individual Olympic athletes.

Media consultants at the international agency Burson Cohn and Wolfe have been surveying the social media presence of leading Olympic sports communities and publish the results in annual reports. The official *@Olympic* counts lead in volume. The IOC's public Twitter account had 6,150,281 followers by the end of 2018. While that is impressive, established sports media with larger staffs remain a step ahead; *L'Equipe*, the leading daily newspaper covering sports in the French language, has 5 million Twitter followers in a country with just 1 percent of the global audience. ESPN is far ahead with 34 million Twitter followers.

A few other Olympic sports organizations are staying ahead in the social media race. Their success underscores the effort involved. Football, basketball, rugby, and cycling have built audiences of millions of followers by investing in dedicated digital media departments. Their success incorporates tried and tested promotions from traditional print and radio media—contests, quizzes, interviews, and guest contributors with large followings of their own. The competition to keep up with demand for content that keeps audiences coming back is demanding—and it is also expensive.

Other sports organizations are finding custom channels a better match for their objectives of growing audiences for their sport and attracting sponsors with loyal viewers. The popular industry jargon for this approach is "OTT." FEI, the International Equestrian Federation, is already well established. In 2015, FEI launched a five-year production partnership with top tier sports promotion agency IMG to create FEI.tv. This subscription service also offers pay-per-view choices. The full-time production organization also generates custom content for a YouTube channel and a monthly print magazine.

The OTT trend gained momentum in 2018, when more federations organizing Olympic sports launched new channels. The International Volleyball Federation launched the FIVB TV channel in partnership with Microsoft with an affordable service starting at under $6. FIH, the Olympic field hockey federation, decided to retain all broadcast rights and use this content for live-streaming to paid subscribers. This was expensive, but the upside of enhancing audience databases made it appealing. The

World Baseball Softball Confederation built a platform for live-streaming select competitions together with Sports Integrated Commercial Solutions. This new resource made it possible to reach baseball fans in countries which had not covered the sport extensively.

The Olympic Channel and sports federation media properties have been able to complement Olympic objectives of knowledge sharing and promoting sports participation. World Sailing broadcasts many events live on its YouTube channel and builds on the attention of viewers to add short tutorials about how to sail and key rules of official sailing competitions. The International Canoe Federation's "Planet Canoe" channel features entire series of video tutorials featuring Olympic athletes' advice. These kinds of learning opportunities provide valuable benefits directly and they also help to maintain viewer interest in the years between the Olympics.

Individual athletes who impress and inspire audiences often have the best success on social media. ISPO, the largest sports industry trade show, distinguished three Winter Olympics champions for their solid followings on Instagram in its 2019 show preview: Martin Fourcade with 376,000, Johannes Thingnes Bö with 166,500, and Laura Dahlmeier with 129,000. The summer sport of volleyball has aimed even higher. Volleyball stars Saied Marouf, Alyssa Valdez, and Bruno Rezende have each surpassed the one-million follower threshold on Instagram.

The most successful Olympic athletes on social media have become more than social media influencers. They stand out as media masters and show how nothing succeeds like success.

A Case in Point: Marcel Hirscher Masters Media

"What I can't do, I can learn," says Austrian ski racer Marcel Hirscher. Three Olympic medals and eight FIS Ski World Cup championship trophies show he had already learned quite a lot by the age of 30.

Hirscher's learning agility helped him to stand out in the media and made him a good match for a new format of magazine taking readers behind the scenes of competitive sports. Red Bulletin Publishing named the magazine "*Heroes*" and launched with a 140-page special issue dedicated to Hirscher.

Red Bulletin recruited Hirscher to be "Team Captain" of publishing the magazine in 2018. The venture is an extension of Hirscher's management talent, which is covered in detail in the magazine itself. In addition to working with sponsors to craft appealing images, Hirscher manages four full-time employees and engages two specialized personal trainers and a professional photographer.

Hirscher's experience with media and communications is a recurring theme. He creates social media content as part of his daily regimen and has well over a half-million followers on both Facebook and Instagram, as well as a quarter-million on Twitter. His unmatched record for winning ski championships has made press conferences and interviews part of his daily life. Public relations expert Stefan Illek and photographer Ronnie Boehm work to strengthen these efforts, but when readers see the sheer volume of communications that Hirscher produces in one publication at one time, he looks as much like a leading media personality as a star athlete.

The credits page shares an overview of the many different media tasks Hirscher manages as part of being a sports personality who values regular communication with fans. Three dozen professionals worked together to craft every detail of the editorial content—writers, photographers, graphic designers, and production assistants. In addition, account managers worked behind the scenes to bring in complementary full-page advertisements and promotions that fit the content and its distinctive "meet the champion" style.

Connecting with fans and keeping their interest is a balancing act. Hirscher and his media team highlight the more average, everyday aspects of Hirscher's life and career to project an image that readers can relate to. Hirscher is in fact average height and weight, 173 cm tall, weighing in at 76 kilograms in the summer. He lives in the county where he grew up, drinks tap water, looks after his son while his wife works, shops at the local mall, and hangs out with two longtime pals, also profiled in the special issue.

There are limits to portraying a decorated Olympic champion as typical and Hirscher's CrossFit regimen photo essay makes this clear with the title: "Do Not Try This at Home." There is more "behind the scenes" content to build a realistic and intriguing picture of the effort involved in becoming a top athlete—and some of the rewards. Readers see Hirscher's fitness regimen, his meticulous planning with equipment supplier Atomic for customized solutions, fulfilling responsibilities to sports organizations, plus the rigors of traveling from race to race, in a way that conventional media reports rarely capture.

"Behind the scenes" is one of several approaches used to engage readers. Other features include human interest, interviews, and a comfortable volume of sponsored content. In a time when audiences are often saturated with brand messages and depend on ad blockers, this approach to working together with sponsors as a team may become a model for brands that seek to maximize their relevance.

While the raffle promotion format is also familiar, the presentation takes sophisticated brand building to the next level and capitalizes on Hirscher's personal brand as an accomplished and likeable sports hero. The invitation to readers to join the contest features a meeting with Marcel Hirscher in person as the first prize and illustrates it with a backdrop showing Hirscher holding a 2018 FIS World Cup trophy with the Audi logo across his chest, dangling Atomic branded goggles and wearing his signature image cap with the logo of his financial sponsor—Raffeisen Bank. The second prize is classically aspirational—a pair of Atomic Redster G9 skis. And there's more—casual clothing from G-Star Raw, Smith performance sunglasses, a Samsung Galaxy watch, a Samsung Galaxy smartphone, and taking readers way behind the scenes, Hirscher's preferred thermal underwear from UYN.

The special issue shows Hirscher taking risks as part of his sporting career, so it is fitting that it tries out different formats which match a risk-taking personality. A "trading places" feature casts a 36-year-old amateur athlete who actually looks like Hirscher as his stand-in. It's a tough job. Doping control officials show up bright and early for a random check, personal trainers push his limits, a physiotherapy session gets his body ready for more. And taking time out for the fans on social media and in person is a must. By evening, the body double, named Josef, is ready to call it a day.

Hirscher opens up about three serious injuries in a way that gives the content authenticity and a balanced perspective distinct from predictable podium appearances. A broken foot, a broken ankle, and injuries from an automobile collision caused by another driver are all part of Hirscher's personal history. His observation, "You talk with ten doctors and you get ten different answers," will resonate with many readers.

A 140-page magazine leaves room for creativity that traditional media projects rarely have. There is "equal time" for Hirscher's rivals, Aksel Lund Svindal and Henrik Kristoffersen. And there is still some time left over for amusement with two comics who poke fun at super-superficial media interviews.

The photo images hark back to the golden era of illustrated magazines before the Internet was flooded with snapshots and selfies. Many are just what you would expect for a race champion—action shots that embody motion and energy. Many other images highlight the human interest aspects and show Hirscher together with a cast of real-life characters that a large audience can relate to personally.

The complete issue shows the kind of talent that helps many top athletes maintain high performance. Strong communications skills, the ability to get the best efforts of others, and a willingness to innovate all stand out in bold. Hirscher adds something important most want, but not all have—a very distinctive and appealing style that has become his personal brand.

Excerpts from "Marcel Hirscher Heroes" are available online in German at: http://info.redbullmediahouse.com/custloads/297852205/md_1076001.pdf

Illustration 6.1 The infrastructure of Olympic Broadcast Services supports the creation of more hours of sports programming than the entire ESPN Network, valued at over $40 billion.

Key Sources and References

beIN Sports Newsroom. August 26, 2016. "4 Olympic Games Exclusive on beIN." Online Publication: https://beinsports.com/en/bein-ioc/

Clarke, S. February 28, 2018. "Discovery and Eurosport Reveal Winter Olympics Numbers in Europe." *Variety*. Online Publication: https://variety.com/2018/tv/news/discovery-eurosport-winter-olympics-total-video-1202710209/

Clover, J. February 26, 2018. "Record Viewership for Olympic Coverage." *Broadband TV News*. Online Publication: https://broadbandtvnews.com/2018/02/27/record-viewership-for-olympic-coverage/

IOC Newsroom. February 28, 2019. "IOC President Bach Outlines Digital Future of the Olympic Games." Online Publication: https://olympic.org/news/ioc-president-bach-outlines-digital-future-of-the-olympic-games

ISPO Newsroom. December 4, 2018. "Sponsors and Successes: The Biathlon Stars of Winter 2018/19." Online Publication: https://ispo.com/en/people/sponsors-and-successes-biathlon-stars-winter-2018/19

Marchal, S. 2019. "Trouver des sponsors grâce au personal branding." *Social Media Workshop at Salon du Running*, Paris, April 13.

Panasonic Newsroom. "Behind the Scenes at the Olympic Games." Online Publication: https://panasonic.com/global/olympic/support.html

Royal Television Society. March 4, 2015. "Olympic Broadcast Progress through Time." Online Publication: https://rts.org.uk/article/olympic-broadcast-progress-through-time

Seven Network Newsroom. October 26, 2018. "Seven Network to Break Olympic Total Audience Records at Tokyo 2020." Online Publication: http://sevenwestmedia.com.au/assets/pdfs/181026-Tokyo-2021.pdf

Vlessing, E. January 19, 2017. "Alibaba to Launch Olympic Sports Streaming Service in China." Online Publication: https://hollywoodreporter.com/news/alibaba-launch-olympic-sports-streaming-service-china-965887

CHAPTER 7

Get Set for 2030

Nothing Succeeds Like Success

Simple movements, repeated intelligently and systematically, build strength for athletic achievement. The Olympic movement reflects this strength. It plays a pivotal role in engaging millions of people to be more active and stay engaged with others who share this goal. It leverages this following to encourage steady improvement to achieve goals. And on its best days, it inspires confidence that accelerates success.

The Olympics has provided a valuable foundation of iconic and universal symbols that resonate in over 200 hundred nations and inspire people from all walks of life. Sometimes the symbols are so prominent that they overshadow the regimens that make the entire Olympic movement possible. These regimens build strength and build expertise that is widely shared through coaching and team efforts in the Olympic tradition.

The benefits of encouraging so many people to improve their physical fitness are substantial—and sometimes the most effective course for counteracting chronic diseases and other maladies. Diplomatic merits such as providing a common interest to bring the two Koreas closer together add to this value.

All benefits have costs. Some cost/benefit evaluations of the Olympic Games look unconvincing. And some individual components of producing the Olympic Games might never return the investments they require. Computing this with the precision of analyzing a bridge or toll road is not possible when many benefits are intangible or unknown until many years in the future.

But it is possible to spotlight individual components of the Olympics that create substantial value to gauge an order of magnitude of how valuable they have become. The multibillion dollar expenses of producing each edition of the Olympic Games make these kinds of comparisons important for discussions about how to plan for the future of the Olympics.

Two benchmarks from major league sports help to show how large the value created by the Olympics has become: team revenues average two times athlete compensation and market values for teams which are sold are typically eight times revenues. Olympic athletes do not receive conventional compensation, but the amounts paid in individual Olympic solidarity scholarships are about $85,000 for one season and top college athletic programs make similar investments. Financial analysts call this kind of measure a "proxy." For all Olympic athletes competing in the Summer and Winter Olympics combined—14,200—this simple estimate of total value is $20 billion. That is a high value by any standard.

Of course, there is much more. Olympic qualifying events, Olympic ceremonies, the Youth Olympic Games, Olympic-affiliated high-performance training centers, documentaries, television series, books, websites, and other media are also assets made possible by the modern Olympic Games.

The very large scale of the Olympics creates a valuable advantage—economies of scale. The economics of high-quality professional video production help to demonstrate the value of this advantage. ESPN Films spent $5 million to produce a seven and a half hour series which won the Oscar for best documentary in 2016. The production cost included storyboards for project planning, research, writing, casting, narration, text and sound overlays, filming, editing, and postproduction quality enhancement. The $5 million budget equates to $667,000 per hour of the completed documentary. The 2016 Summer Olympics supported the production of 357,000 hours of high-quality original video for ESPN Latin America and other official broadcasters. These assets would have cost $238 billion to create if the expenditure level was comparable to ESPN Films for an individual project such as the Oscar award winning documentary. Total television production costs at Rio 2016 were in the billions of dollars, but just a small fraction of $238 billion, because the infrastructure of the Olympics venues and International Broadcast Center was shared by over 60 broadcasters and a large part of the research and preparation was provided by Olympic Broadcasting Services.

The total operating costs for Rio 2016 were finalized at $13.2 billion. When the accounts were tallied up, revenues covered the expenses, but $13.2 billion is a large amount for 17 days of sports events and ceremonies plus a year of test events. It is more than $1,000 per resident of the Rio de Janeiro metropolitan region. But it is a modest amount compared to typical costs for producing 357,000 hours of high-quality original video.

The Olympics also earn a premium for audience aggregation. The large premium marketing professionals have been paying for NFL Super Bowl ads in the United States reflects this. The NFL Super Bowl is seen by about one-third of the entire population in the United States. The price for one minute of advertising broadcast nationwide was more than $10 million in 2018 to reach an audience of 107 million viewers. Conventional advertising campaigns to reach as many viewers through many different programs collectively cost less than one-fifth of this benchmark.

Reaching an audience 32 times larger than the U.S. audience for the Super Bowl during the Summer Olympics does not create $320 million per minute in value because most advertising rates are lower outside the United States. But this comparison shows that if the global audience watched the Summer Olympics an hour each day during the 17-day event schedule, the commercial value of this attention would approach $325 billion. This type of comparison is one reason that marketing experts often estimate the value of the Olympics brand between $30 billion and $40 billion. Olympic organizations and athletes only share part of this value since many broadcasters, sports federations, National Olympic Committees (NOCs), local hosts, and production contractors share in both the costs and the benefits.

Not all of the value created by the Olympics is purely economic. One of its greatest achievements has been to inspire the organization of 600 other international multisport competitions in two decades and 600 more in the previous century. These events help achieve other goals. The World Master's Games promotes lifelong physical fitness. The Paralympics adapts sports practices for people with disabilities to help them live healthier and more rewarding lives.

Participation at the Ninth IOC Athletes Commission Forum in April 2019 helps to illustrate how extensive the reach of the Olympic movement has become; 350 athlete representatives took part. They worked together on behalf of hundreds of affiliates:

- 185 NOCs
- 50 International Federations (IFs)
- Five continental Athletes Commissions (ACs)
- ACs of all the Organizing Committees of the upcoming Olympic Games
- International Paralympic Committee (IPC)
- World Anti-Doping Agency (WADA)
- World Olympians Association (WOA)

There are many more Olympic affiliated associations, such as the Olympic Museums Network, the League of Olympic Cities, and the Association of Presidents of National Olympic Committees. Collectively, the constellation of international multisport competitions reinforces many of the strengths that have made the modern Olympics a success story:

- Providing high-performance athletic training to tens of thousands of participants who can share their expertise with teammates and are better prepared to become trainers and coaches
- Promoting a culture of volunteerism and development of management expertise that enhances the contributions of volunteers
- Building communities of fans with common interests and promoting sociability
- Providing a showcase for the culture and talent of the host region and country
- Offering forums for international communication and dialog
- Providing interesting content for educational programs and advancing health and human performance education
- Providing a testing ground for innovative technologies and communications programs

These benefits all have one factor in common. They are *worldwide*. When Rossignol works with Olympic medalist Martin Fourcade to develop superior lightweight insulated jackets or other high-performance gear, these products are available to customers from every nation. The educational outreach programs developed by the Olympic education department are available to schools around the globe. Citizens of every country can register for online courses from the IOC Athlete Learning Gateway. Most sessions of the International Olympic Academy are streamed live online. Most high-performance sports training complexes affiliated with the Olympics accommodate athletes from other countries. Omega's precision measurement technologies developed for Olympic competitions are available everywhere. Viewers worldwide can watch Olympic sports competitions and ceremonies on television and see many recordings online.

The worldwide reach of the Olympics is an impressive achievement. But this success is now testing some limits of its own. Historically, most of the operating expenditures and almost all construction for the Olympics have been funded by partnerships based in the host city. Some multinational corporations also help out with contributions. Nissan joined three Brazilian corporations in the top tier of official sponsors of Rio 2016. All of the Tokyo 2020 Gold Partners are based in Japan, but two of the second tier of Olympic official partners are based overseas—Cisco from the United States and EF Education of Switzerland. Ticket revenues and hotel taxes used to cover more of the expenses, but these have not kept up with annual cost increases averaging 11 percent. So as the success of the Olympics has grown, the resources required of host cities have grown too. For some potential host cities, this growth has been too much.

The Price of Success

Financial professionals frequently refer to a negative factor that is out of the ordinary at a successful enterprise as a "red flag." The Olympics has one. It is too big to overlook. The vacancy rate of voting positions on the International Olympic Committee is very high. In early 2019, 20 of the 115 positions were vacant. Athletes whose results are that far from their targets never win.

In addition, participation by IOC voting members is much less than 100 percent. Only 84 votes were cast on July 31, 2015, when the voting members of the IOC selected Beijing to host the 2022 Winter Olympic

Games. Fifteen voting members did not participate and 16 positions were vacant.

The Olympic tradition of being a volunteer managed organization may have outlived its usefulness. Las Vegas, founded a decade after the Olympics, had a volunteer Fire Department until 1942, when its population passed the 10,000 mark. After the workload exceeded the capacities of a volunteer organization, the city hired full-time firefighters and managers. Of course, the IOC employs over 500 professionals to manage daily operations and liaisons with other sports organizations and supporters. But there is rarely independent staff support for IOC voting members although their responsibilities are comparable to corporate directors and legislators with large budgets for capable independent advisors.

Working together with Olympic medalists, cabinet ministers, and other political heavyweights, as well as the heads of large global organizations, requires exceptional credentials, skill, and powers of persuasion. The pool of talent is limited and often recruited for roles as directors at other organizations, television show hosts, keynote speakers, political committee chairs, or other leadership positions. Unlike the community of Olympic athletes, there are no designated alternates and there is no development program to build a candidate pool large enough to meet future needs.

The Olympics also has a continuing challenge to improve public understanding of the actual costs of presenting the Olympics and its benefits, as well as the large number of communities which benefit. Nearly 5 million viewers have seen a six-minute mini-documentary from *Business Insider* called "Why Hosting the Olympics Isn't Worth It Anymore" on YouTube. It included the frequently cited and controversial figure of $51 billion in expenditures for the 2014 Winter Olympic Games in Sochi. The operational accounts of Sochi 2014 actually reported a modest surplus, which was used to customize a Russian language version of the Olympic Channel.

The very large construction expenditures at Sochi 2014 reflected economic factors that only a few financial professionals who rate government debt ever discuss. Russia has exceptionally low government debt rates—about 20 percent of annual economic output compared to 100 percent for the United States and 250 percent for Japan. Very low government debt rates can trigger damaging deflationary cycles or constrain institutions like pension funds and foundations which must allocate a certain amount of their assets to government bonds. Government borrowing to make very large infrastructure expenditures for the 2014 Olympics and 2018 World Cup was one of just a few choices in this unusual economic environment.

The construction expenditures for Sochi 2014 were comparable to the cost of building the University of California. Many Sochi 2014 facilities were converted to become the new campus of Russia International Olympic University. This detail is downright boring compared to a provocative headline like "Why Hosting the Olympics Isn't Worth It Anymore." Olympic leaders have faced a big challenge in overcoming damage from widely viewed reports like this which overlook important economic factors.

These issues are causing expensive challenges of their own. In April 2019, a city council representative from the Paris municipal government, Danielle Simonnet, called for a public referendum about canceling the Paris 2024 Summer Olympics. She argued that investments in public transit and improving the environment were higher priorities. The background information she cited was imprecise, but just the kind of report that can raise objections. A mobile carrier used a polling app to poll some of its subscribers on a random basis and 62 percent of those responding favored cancellation.

Competition is a key element of Olympic sports and competing successfully for public resources is also important. Many other kinds of long-term investments merit consideration—public health research and communications, public broadcasting, public libraries, public schools, public transit, roads, highways, bridges, and tunnels, to name a few. But the mathematics of diversification make it important for sports and fitness facilities to be included in these investment portfolios. Over long terms of 30 years or more, a portfolio that is concentrated in just a few areas always underperforms a portfolio that is better diversified.

The long list of challenges the Olympics face in the next decade should include an up-to-date look at sports gambling following the industry's explosive growth. According to Zion Market Research, total expenditures on sports betting surpassed $100 billion per year for the first time in

2017. This analysis projected 9 percent annual growth through 2024, following a U.S. Supreme Court decision in May 2018 which permitted individual states to legalize sports betting. The sports betting industry has reached a revenue level comparable to Bank of China or JP Morgan Chase, two of the world's largest banks.

In the past decade, sports betting has only produced costs and administrative burdens for the Olympics, with no measurable benefits. In 2008, the IOC established an "Integrity Betting Intelligence System" designed to alert authorities to any unusual patterns in sports betting which might uncover unfair manipulation of competitions. Results from London 2012 showed that the technology and alert procedures worked and no criminal activity took place.

One of the most notorious cases of match fixing involving Olympic athletes also showed that monitoring can work dependably and the spirit of resilience that is a recurring theme in Olympic sports can help misguided athletes refocus on sports after they have been disciplined. In a plot more like the script of a lighthearted comedy than a crime scene investigation, a pizza parlor manager persuaded nine players of the Montpellier Handball team to underperform in competition with a lower ranked opponent so that bets favoring the opponent would yield big gains. The volume of total bets placed on the October 2012 match was 40 times levels typical for this matchup and over 99 percent favored Montpelier's lower ranked opponent. French gambling authorities were alerted immediately. They investigated and turned in the suspects for prosecution.

The criminal defendants included Nikola Karabatic, the captain of France's Olympic handball team, and his brother Luca, also a player on the French National Team. They were found guilty of fraud, fined 10,000 Euros each and given suspended sentences of two months. The French Handball Federation suspended Nikola for six games and Luca for two. After Nikola returned to playing handball, he won the IHF Player of the Year Award in 2016, as well as an Olympic silver medal as a player on the French National Team. Both brothers were recruited to play for Paris Saint-Germain Handball and won the 2018 Eurotournoi championship together with their teammates.

Some business contacts with the sports betting industry in the future appear inevitable for the Olympics. FDJ Group, a leader in the sports betting industry, was an official partner of the Paris 2024 bid. It is char-tered as a foundation and distributes its surplus to promote education and cultural activities. The FDJ Group has ambitions to operate worldwide.

In addition, Olympic TOP sponsor VISA ranks as the single most widely accepted means of payment in the online sports gambling indus-try. According to thorough research by the European Commission and the French Institute for International and Strategic Affairs, VISA payments are accepted by 86 percent of 3,620 sports gambling websites surveyed.

The Olympics also faces challenges and opportunities in the world's second most populous country, India. The fee Sony Pictures Network paid to secure broadcast rights in India for the Tokyo 2020 Olympics was just $12 million. That is less than one cent for each of India's 1.3 billion residents. By contrast, Eurosport paid $1.5 billion for Olympic broadcast rights from 2018 to 2024 covering European markets with a population just one-third of India. India's Star Sports Network, which had paid $20 million for the broadcast rights from 2014 to 2016, declined the rights for Tokyo 2020 and Sony Pictures Network did not seek an option for Beijing 2022.

India is on track to surpass China as the world's most populous country in the next decade, but it is far behind China in Olympic sports activities. Athletes from India won 3 medals at Beijing 2008, 1 gold and 2 bronze, while athletes from China won 100, including 48 gold medals. At London 2012, athletes from India won 2 silver and 4 bronze medals for a total of 6, compared to 91 for China, of which 38 were gold. India's results at Rio 2016 took a step backwards with just 1 silver and 1 bronze medal each, while China achieved a total of 70. India took home no medals at all from the 2018 Winter Olympics.

Sports are popular in India, where the sport of choice is cricket, a sport much like field hockey in Olympic sports. India's showdown with Pakistan in the ICC Champions Trophy series ranked as the most viewed program in India in 2017 with an audience of 72 million. Cricket players in India's Men's Premier League earn the highest compensation per match of professional athletes in any team sport, more than $350,000. That is almost twice the per match compensation paid to professionals in the NFL. Nonetheless, India has not won an Olympic medal in men's field hockey since 1980 and the national women's field hockey team did not qualify for the Olympics from 1984 through 2012. No Olympic athlete or team ranked in the top 10 list of sports sponsorships and licenses in India compiled by *InsideSport*, India's leading sports business publication.

The Olympics has great upside potential in India if it can follow a good game plan. There is a good reason this should be a high priority. By 2030, India will account for over one-fifth of the world's university student population. It is positioned to have an influential role in education worldwide. India's Patiala high-performance sports training center, managed by the Sports Authority of India, is the largest in Asia with facilities for 1,000 athletes and can accommodate visiting athletes and coaches from foreign countries. The Master of Science in Coaching and postgraduate sports medicine programs for doctors admit candidates from all over the world.

A Healthy Outlook

The convergence of the sports world with the field of health and human performance has good upside potential for the Olympics and its ecosystem. Sports promotion programs that may have looked expensive in the past can look good in comparison to expensive medical treatments that take many years to develop and test.

Cystic fibrosis treatments illustrate this dramatically. The standard price for Vertex Orkambi, an approved treatment which is considered suitable for about 40 percent of patients diagnosed with the disease, is about $135,000 per year. Vigorous athletic training regimens cost much less and have helped many cystic fibrosis patients avoid early death.

The World Health Organization recently described antibiotic resistance as a "global health emergency." The ecosystem of sports and human performance expertise that has developed around the Olympics is just one resource for responding effectively to this crisis. But it may be the only resource that can be mobilized worldwide through networks of participants who have extensive experience working together and achieving common goals.

The unique network which has developed around the Association of Sport Performance Centres (ASPC) works closely with NOCs. The association has become the "Premier League" of sports technology and performance education. It is also a role model for knowledge sharing in the Olympic and Paralympic movements. The 88 centers are advancing their capabilities in injury prevention and recovery, as well as programs for athletes with disabilities. As the sports industry plays a greater role in promoting health and human performance knowhow, this network is positioned to become a more valuable asset which can promote better health around the world.

The Olympic tradition of knowledge sharing is accelerating the importance of ASPC institutes in promoting health and human performance excellence for the general public. Most provide top-notch facilities to the public on a fee basis. They also share experience working with high-performance athletes in conferences open to sports industry professionals, and publish websites, magazines, and books. INSEP, the ASPC member in France, has an entire department dedicated to producing books, magazines, newsletters, websites, and webcasts. Important ASPC institute topics covered include strength conditioning, physical literacy, body composition analysis, sports nutrition, and injury prevention.

A 2017 survey of ASPC members showed extensive development of sports science expertise. Participants whose national Olympic teams ranked in the Top 20 at the Rio 2016 Olympics all manage sports medicine and physiotherapy practices. Most also have general practitioners, chiropractors, and osteopaths working with the sports medicine team. Expertise in sports science was also strong. All Top 20 group respondents engage experts in exercise physiology, sports psychology, video performance analysis, and athletic conditioning, while almost all incorporate biomechanics and sports nutrition in their sport science programs.

Other programs managed by ASPC members have assembled a very broad range of capabilities in applying sport science. The list includes cryotherapy, sport engineering, trauma center management, and integrated recovery services. The entire Rio 2016 Top 20 tier surveyed provide athletes with sophisticated recovery services.

Integrated sports performance and injury recovery facilities are a valuable addition to the array of choices available to improve human health and performance. The increasing seriousness of some sports related injuries which have made this important detracts from the value created by the Olympic movement. More athletes died from injuries at cricket matches in the decade from 2005 to 2015 than in the entire 20th century. The NFL reported that the total of player concussions reported rose from 206 in 2014 to 281 in 2017. The concussion rate in NFL style tackle football is about 15 percent lower than in rugby, considered the most dangerous sport, according to Complete Concussion Management, a network of clinics based in Canada.

Sports science is positioned to push back against unfavorable trends in sports safety. From Torino 2006 to Sochi 2014 the FIS Alpine skiing World Cup series reported 726 injuries. Only 500 athletes compete in a typical season, so the risk of injury is very high. New airbag technologies designed for skiers are showing promising results. Italian sportswear innovator Dainese adapted airbag equipped jackets first developed for motorcyclists for ski racers and became the first vendor to win FIS product testing certification in this category. Patented textile technology fine tunes the safety gear to minimize the risk of injury. Austrian Olympic champion Matthias Meyer demonstrated the product's effectiveness when he crashed in a race in December 2015.

The economies of scale demonstrated by the Olympics in broadcasting may become an asset in reversing unfavorable trends in sports injuries. ISPO, the world's largest sports equipment exhibition, showcased dozens of promising technological innovations to promote sports safety at its most recent show in 2019. Standouts featured impressive innovations:

- *TriEye* won the ISPO Gold Award for 2019 with new performance sunglasses incorporating a compact rear view screen in the corner of one lens. This innovation was originally designed for cyclists, but also has excellent potential for applications across the field of health and human performance.
- *Uvex* is showing how athlete safety technologies can have much wider benefits. Its research and development team engineers both sports safety products for athletes and industrial safety products for manufacturing and construction. Uvex helmets, goggles, clothing, gloves, and lightweight running shoes are developed with input from a thousand athletes and regularly improved to combine athletic performance with protection from injuries.

- *Flaxta* designs helmets and wearable protective clothing which incorporate sensors to measure impacts or concussions and identify impacts which need medical attention. Flaxta sports clothes incorporate meshes of shock absorbers to reduce risk of injury and the firm's goggles incorporate lens technology which enhances ability to see contrasts. Both features can be adapted to uses for workplace safety and public safety.

Collectively, the dozens of sports safety innovators at ISPO demonstrate that many Olympic sports are providing the critical mass to cover the research and development costs of new products that can also improve health and safety of the general public. The economies of scale which the global scale of the Olympics has created is helping to build a legacy of helping humans everywhere live longer, healthier, and safer lives.

A Human Race

Health and human performance expertise are promoting a healthy outlook for the Olympics. This is critical during the current period of ongoing challenges and confusion caused by continuing doping and other banned performance enhancements in sports. The challenge is serious and involves so many different authorities in different countries that a quick solution would be the ultimate "impossible moment" in Olympic history.

Several studies show that nonconforming drug test results are almost two-thirds lower for Olympic athletes than for professional athletes in non-Olympic sports. The layers of bureaucracy of national sports federations, NOCs, IFs, Olympic qualifying event staffs, customs agents, multiple health authorities, and law enforcement organizations are cumbersome. But at a minimum, this level of attention has some effectiveness as a deterrent.

Sophisticated applications of artificial intelligence may be able to consolidate the collective experience of many authorities working to detect and correct improper use of performance enhancements in Olympic sports. It has not been possible to obtain insurance for manipulation of competition through banned performance enhancements in the past.

There was not enough data and there were too many uncertainties. At the rate technology is progressing, insurance solutions should be possible in the future.

The diversity of skills in the talent pool of the Olympic community can support solutions for many challenges that face the Olympics and host cities. The topic of biodiversity has earned much attention and deserves it. Biodiversity can impact the world's capacity to produce critical food and medicine products in the future. For similar reasons, skills diversity deserves attention, too. Science, technology, engineering, and math, often labeled STEM, have many advocates in education and government. But these skills alone cannot manage all the challenges facing the world today. Communications skills, team management skills, agility, resilience, and other foundations of the Olympics are also important. The challenges of the coming decade can put Olympic human resources to work and help to educate a new generation.

The Olympics is already promoting global skills diversity with two large initiatives. The IOC's Athlete Learning Gateway for online courses presented by leading experts is available to everyone who registers, not just Olympic affiliates. Earning a gold medal in the program requires effort and improvement, just as in the Olympic Games. And as Olympic volunteer programs have grown in step with the Olympic Games, online and personal training for volunteers has achieved the sophistication of corporate training programs. Many Olympic volunteers return for future editions of the Games and share their experience with new recruits.

What direction will the Olympics move in the future? What new challenges will arise? Which personalities will become legends worthy of the best Olympic traditions? No one knows for sure—that alone keeps the discussion lively and makes the Olympics a center of attention around the globe.

The Olympic community was treated to an optimistic perspective at the ceremony celebrating the graduation of the class of 2018 at AiSTS. This Masters of Sports Management program was launched in 2001 by the IOC in partnership with the University of Geneva and graduate schools in Lausanne. Its graduates have reinforced the strategic foundations of the Olympics: building on tradition, adapting to a changing world, and providing leadership for the future.

The 40 graduates in the class of 2018, from 26 different countries, were joined by relatives, friends, fellow alumni, and well-wishers from around the world. They were all accomplished athletes who also excelled in school and advanced the program's founding goal—to promote professionalism in sports with the support of technology and sports science.

IOC President Thomas Bach congratulated each graduate in person and shared a brief talk, speaking as a colleague and as a friend of the sports community. He finished where the Olympic story began, with values so enduring the world embraces them 28 centuries after the first Olympic contests were held in Olympia in ancient Greece.

Bach reminded the graduates that the world around them is changing every day and encouraged them to "look at this with a spirit of looking for opportunities." He observed "the Olympic values still have an impact in this world. These values are not exactly what people are promoting as the values of today. Look at politics—look at business—you don't find much respect at all." He promoted the view that "dialogue is the basis of sport," reflected by a slide show of the graduates exchanging ideas in the classroom and at sports trials. He concluded, "Look at this with a view that you can promote the values to a bright future."

How bright will this future shine? A replica of an Olympic cauldron illuminated the entry to the International Olympic Museum where the ceremony took place. It reminded all how meaningful and enduring the universal symbols of the Olympics remain, even as the world around us changes every day.

As each graduate moved across the stage with the spirit of accomplishment we see on Olympic podiums a slide with a phrase each chose to inspire the community illuminated the auditorium. Sports media entrepreneur Rita Pivoriunaite of Lithuania, a six-time European champion in karate, summed up the experience with a simple, inspiring phrase—"I can. I will. The End."

Illustration 7.1 Surrounded by iconic images of the Olympic movement at the International Olympic Museum, IOC President Thomas Bach encouraged young sports business experts to aspire to a bright future.

Key Sources and References

"Consensus Statement on Concussion in Sport: The 5th International Conference."

Badenhausen, K. July 22, 2019. "The World's 50 Most Valuable Sports Teams 2019." Published Online: https://forbes.com/sites/kurtbadenhausen/2019/07/22/the-worlds-50-most-valuable-sports-teams-2019/#75dc6af8283d

Bell, D. November 2011. *Encyclopedia of International Games*. McFarland Books.

Berlin, April 28, 2017. Published Online: https://completeconcussions.com/2017/04/28/consensus-statement-concussion-sport/

Boseley, S., and R. Davies. 2019. "Firm in NHS Row Over Cystic Fibrosis." *The Guardian*, March 6.

Business Insider Staff. February 5, 2018. "Why Hosting The Olympics Isn't Worth It Anymore." Published Online: https://youtube.com/watch?v=0bXJGZgR1BU

Davis, P., and D. Henwood. January 24, 2019. "Functionality and Capability of High Performance Training Centres (HPTCs) – 2017." Pamphlet, Association Sport Performance Centres.

Etchells, D. April 8, 2019. "Paris 2024 Dismiss Call from City Councillor for Referendum on Whether to Cancel Olympic Games." *Inside the Games*.

Published Online: https://insidethegames.biz/articles/1077737/paris-2024-dismiss-call-from-city-councillor-for-referendum-on-whether-to-cancel-olympic-games

European Commission and the French Institute for International and Strategic Affairs (IRIS). June 2017. "Preventing Criminal Risks Linked to the Sports Betting Market." Published Online: http://iris-france.org/wp-content/uploads/2017/06/PRECRIMBET_2017_FINAL.pdf

Handball Planet Editor. February 2, 2018. "Fines for Brothers Karabatic and Five More Players for Betting-Scandal." *Handball Planet*. Published Online: http://handball-planet.com/fines-for-brothers-karabatic-and-five-more-players-for-betting-scandal/

Ingle, S. 2019. "Cricket Insurance Booms after Players Scramble to Protect IPL Riches." *The Guardian*, March 21.

International Olympic Committee. 2017. "Marketing Report Rio 2016."

IOC Newsroom. April 14, 2019. "Biggest Ever International Athletes Forum."

IOC Newsroom. July 2019. "Members." Published Online: https://olympic.org/ioc-members-list

IOC Official Website. June 2019. "Organizations Recognized by the International Olympic Committee." Published Online: https://olympic.org/ioc-governance-affiliate-organisations

ISPO Munich. February 2019. "Official Catalog 2019." Messe Munich.

John, J. December 24, 2018. "Global Sports Betting Market Will Reach USD 155.49 Billion By 2024: Zion Market Research." Published Online: https://globenewswire.com/news-release/2018/12/24/1678117/0/en/Global-Sports-Betting-Market-Will-Reach-USD-155-49-Billion-By-2024-Zion-Market-Research.html

Kansal, S. 2019. "IOC, SPN Confirm Tokyo 2020 Olympics Broadcast Deal." *InsideSport India*, March 14.

Reuters News. October 1, 2012. "Karabatic Involved in Betting Probe: Prosecutor." Published Online: https://reuters.com/article/us-handball-france-montpellier/karabatic-involved-in-betting-probe-prosecutor-idUSBRE8900L420121001

Sporting News Editors, February 4, 2019. "Super Bowl 53 commercials: How Much Do Ads cost in 2019?" Published Online: https://msn.com/en-au/news/other/super-bowl-53-commercials-how-much-do-ads-cost-in-2019/ar-BBT8BJU

WADA. July 24, 2018. "2017 Anti-Doping Testing Figures." World Anti-Doping Agency.

Key Terms

Accelerator/Incubator: provider of shared support services for newly founded or early-stage enterprises with high growth potential

Capital expenditures: financial outlays for physical infrastructure projects or major improvements to existing projects related to presentation of sports events

International Sports Federation: officially recognized international organization which exercises exclusive rights to organize Olympic qualifying events and also operates multiple programs designed to promote participation in its sport

National Olympic Committee: officially recognized national organization which selects athletes and manages preparations for Olympic competitions in an individual country such as Mexico or a territory which independently administers public education, such as Puerto Rico

Olympic movement: interconnected community of independent organizations which promote Olympic values and ideas and invite broad participation

Professional athlete: athletic competitor whose primary source of income is derived from salaries, bonuses, prize money, commercial sponsorships, and grants for participation in sports events

Sports franchise: the business activities and brand programs related to a sports team or sports event series which add financial value

Sports science: application of scientific knowledge to measure and improve sports performance

Venture capital: private equity investment made by professional investment organizations which build portfolios of private investments and seek to sell their shares after investment companies have established a track record of profitability

About the Author

Max Donner is a private equity investment analyst and widely published author of magazine features and interviews. He began his publishing career as a stock market columnist and followed reader interest to add two decades of in-depth sports business coverage. He studied economics at Amherst College and Cornell University and finance at Harvard Business School, where he was awarded an MBA degree with honors.

Foreword author **Steve Wilson** has covered Olympic sports for Associated Press and the *Olympic Review* and was President of the Society of Olympic Journalists through 2018.

Index

OTHER TITLES IN THE SPORTS AND ENTERTAINMENT MANAGEMENT AND MARKETING COLLECTION

Lynn Kahle, University of Oregon, Editor

- *Artist Development Essentials* by Hristo Penchev
- *Great Coaching and Your Bottom Line* by Marijan Hizak

Announcing the Business Expert Press Digital Library

Concise e-books business students need for classroom and research

This book can also be purchased in an e-book collection by your library as

- a one-time purchase,
- that is owned forever,
- allows for simultaneous readers,
- has no restrictions on printing, and
- can be downloaded as PDFs from within the library community.

Our digital library collections are a great solution to beat the rising cost of textbooks. E-books can be loaded into their course management systems or onto students' e-book readers.
The **Business Expert Press** digital libraries are very affordable, with no obligation to buy in future years. For more information, please visit **www.businessexpertpress.com/librarians**. To set up a trial in the United States, please email **sales@businessexpertpress.com**.

www.ingramcontent.com/pod-product-compliance
Lightning Source LLC
Chambersburg PA
CBHW061307220326
41599CB00026B/4776